HAIDA ART

HAIDA ART

GEORGE F. MacDONALD

Douglas & McIntyre
Vancouver/Toronto

Canadian Museum of Civilization
Hull, Quebec

PLATE 1A, 1B (opening pages)
A complex transformation mask.
Closed, the mask depicts a
Whale with a Seagull on its head
(*left*, PLATE 1A). When the
Whale's face is opened, the dorsal fin and the gull's head both
fold back to reveal the humanlike inner face (*right*, PLATE 1B).
Copper eyebrows, lips and cheek
decorations complete this mask.
*Collected on Haida Gwaii in 1879
by Israel W. Powell.* CMC VII-B-23
(s92-4172 closed, s92-4174 open)

PLATE 2 (frontispiece)
A pair of interior house posts
from Grizzly Bear House, which
belonged to Chief Xa'na of
Masset. Richard Maynard notes
in his log for 1884 that he assembled these items, including the
war daggers and model totem
poles, when the residents of
Masset refused to pose for him.
The large posts, collected by the
Berlin Museum, were removed
to East Germany at the end of
World War II, but are now in
the Dahlem Museum, Berlin.
*Photograph by Richard
Maynard, 1884.* CMC 100462

Douglas & McIntyre Ltd.
1615 Venables Street
Vancouver, British Columbia V5L 2H1

Published simultaneously in the United States of America by University of Washington Press

CANADIAN CATALOGUING IN PUBLICATION DATA

MacDonald, George F.

    Haida art
    ISBN 1-55054-402-0

1. Haida Indians—Art. 2. Indians of North America—British
Columbia—Queen Charlotte Islands—Art. I. Title.
E99.H2M32 1996   730'.89'972   C95-911253-7

Editing by Saeko Usukawa
Design by Barbara Hodgson
Design assistance by Val Speidel
Map by Isabelle Swiderski
Front cover photograph of mask of a young woman wearing a small
    labret of abalone shell, collected on Haida Gwaii in 1879 by Israel W. Powell,
    CMC VII-B-928A (s85-3284), by Harry Foster
Back cover photograph of frontlet depicting a young woman, carved by Simeon Stiltla,
    collected at Masset before 1884 by Dr. William F. Tolmie, CMC VII-B-25 (s86-3275),
    by Harry Foster
Publication co-ordination at Canadian Museum of Civilization by Cathrine Wanczycki
French translation by Christian Berubé
Printed and bound in Canada by Hemlock Printers Ltd.
Printed on acid-free paper ∞

The publisher gratefully acknowledges the assistance of the Canada Council and of the
British Columbia Ministry of Tourism, Small Business and Culture.

CONTENTS

Preface   ix

CHAPTER 1   FROM TIME IMMEMORIAL   3

PREHISTORY OF HAIDA GWAII   3

SOCIAL ORGANIZATION   6

MYTHOLOGY AND CRESTS   7

ART   9

    The North Coast Art Style   9

    Flat Design   12

    Sculpture   13

CHAPTER 2   GIFTS OF THE RAVEN   15

CHIEFLY POSSESSIONS   15

    Clothing (Chilkat Blankets; Painted Leather Capes; Tunics,   16
        Dance Aprons and Leggings; Button Blankets)

    Headdresses (Frontlets, Painted Woven Hats)   23

    Raven Rattles   31

    Copper Shields   31

HOSTING THE FEAST   37

    Ladles and Horn Spoons   37

    Food Dishes and Bowls   43

    Bentwood Trays and Serving Dishes   44

CHAPTER 3   THE SUPERNATURAL WORLD   53

SHAMANISM   53

SECRET SOCIETIES   67

MASKS   71

LUCK OF THE GAMBLER   92

SMOKE FEASTS FOR THE ANCESTORS   94

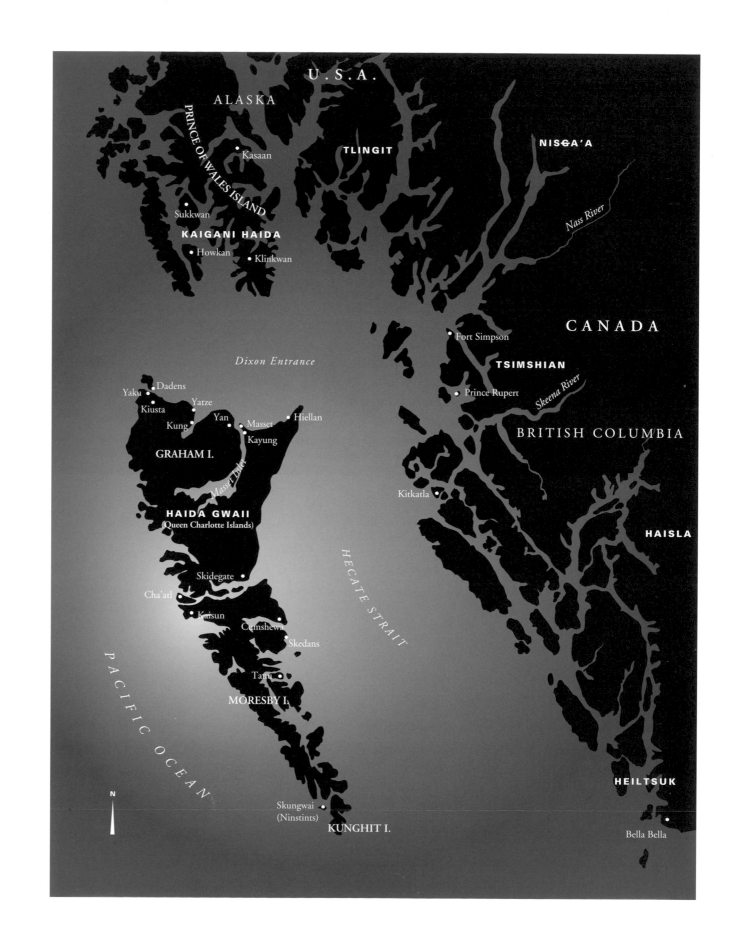

PREHISTORY OF HAIDA GWAII

Haida Gwaii is an archipelago of islands (the Queen Charlotte Islands) off the northern coast of British Columbia near the province's border with Alaska (PLATE 3). The southern islands are mountainous, with Moresby Island predominating. The large northern island, Graham Island, where the Haida people now live, is mountainous on its western side but to the east is flat with isolated outcrops of rock. North of Dixon Entrance are the Kaigani Haida, as the Haida in Alaska are named. Their territory encompasses the southern half of Prince of Wales Island in Alaska.

During the end of the last ice age between 13,000 and 11,000 years ago, events resulted in very low water levels around Haida Gwaii. What is now Hecate Strait, the body of water that separates Haida Gwaii from the mainland, was for the most part dry land. Throughout this area of dry land, there were lakes and small rivers draining north and south to the Pacific Ocean. Soil samples from Hecate Strait indicate that many areas were habitable in the last ice age. After 10,000 years ago, the melting glaciers contributed to a rise in the sea level that resulted in a flooding of the Northwest Coast, temporarily creating beach lines high above today's high tide marks.

The memory of this drastic fluctuation of sea levels is preserved in the widespread flood myths of people along the Northwest Coast. Scores of these stories have been recorded. In 1892, James Deans, a Hudson's Bay Company employee, was told a legend that was very specific about glacial events at the Honna River on Haida Gwaii (1899:67):

> This is the story of the long long ago told amongst our people, the Hidery, that at Quilh-cah about three miles west from the village of Illth-cah-geetla, or Skidegate's town, lived a boy whose name was Scannah-gan-nuncus . . .
>
> . . . One day, making a further venture than usual, he sailed up the Hunnah, a mountain stream emptying its waters into Skidegate channel, four or five miles [6.5 to 8 km.] west from the place where he lived.
>
> Tradition says that this river in those days was three times larger than it is nowadays. At present there is seldom water enough to float a canoe, unless at high water. It is also related that the waters of the sea stood higher on the land than is now the case. Of the rise of the land, evidence is everywhere to be seen; old landmarks show thirty feet [9 m].

PLATE 3

Map of Haida Gwaii (the Queen Charlotte Islands) and Kaigani Haida territory on Prince of Wales Island.

After pulling up stream, he became tired; so, in order to rest, he pulled ashore and lay down. In those days at the place where he went ashore were large boulders in the bed of the stream, while on both sides of the river were many trees. While resting by the river, he heard a dreadful noise up stream, coming toward him. Looking to see what it was, he was surprised to behold all the stones in the river coming toward him. The movement of the stones frightened him so much that he jumped to his feet and ran into the timber. Here he found he had made a mistake, because all the trees were cracking and groaning; all seemed to say to him, "Go back, go back at once to the river, and run as fast as you can." This he lost no time doing. When again at the river, led by his curiosity, he went to see what was crushing the stones and breaking the trees. On reaching them, he found that a large body of ice was coming down, pushing everything before it. Seeing this, he got into his canoe and fled toward home.

Deans speculates, with some insight, on a problem that still puzzles us today (1899:70-71):

Who was the author of this story, or when was it adopted by the Scannahs [Killer Whale phratry], I cannot say. Doubtless a tradition of ice coming down the Hunnah was current at the time when the Scannahs chose that fish as their crest. This event must have happened very early in the settlement of these islands, for tradition says at the time only two or three families lived on the southeast side of these islands, and that, excepting our hero and his grandmother, who lived at Quilh-cah, all the others dwelt in a small village on Maud Island, a mile and a half west from the others at Quilh-cah.

According to Haida tradition, there was a remnant of an earlier population on the west coast of Haida Gwaii. Marius Barbeau of the Canadian Museum of Civilization collected a flood legend from Henry Young of Skidegate (Barbeau, no date:MS). Intensive review of the body of flood and related myths of the Haida is likely to prove that they have inhabited Haida Gwaii since the end of the last ice age and thus constitute one of the oldest traceable populations of any in the New World.

The first indications of the Haida presence consist of roughly flaked stone tools found in intertidal areas that were once dry land. Ocean-going canoes enabled these earliest inhabitants to communicate with neighbours to the north, from whom they adopted new forms of tools such as sharp stone flakes called microblades. These were preferably made of obsidian, a volcanic glass that can be precisely fingerprinted to identify its place of origin. The presence on the islands of obsidian from mainland sources long distances away provides a clue to the maritime skills of the ancient people of Haida Gwaii.

Archaeological surveys have located sites in all parts of Haida Gwaii that indicate the population was sizable by 5,000 years ago. At about that time, their economy was expanding from a primary reliance on hunting and fishing to include harvesting shellfish from the huge intertidal areas that surround many of the more protected waterways of the islands. The abundance of shellfish provided a virtually inexhaustible supply of food; it also made possible a stability of residence that allowed the establishment of more permanent villages where food, tools and other material objects could be safely stored, as well as the development of craftsmen who could devote more time to art. These changes led to the refinement of woodworking tools and skills, which, in turn, allowed for the construction of bigger and more elaborate canoes as well as larger plank houses.

Improved watercraft also meant that people were able to travel to food resources in far-flung areas and that warfare, particularly against mainland tribes, was a profitable venture. In fact, at the time of first contact with Europeans, the Haida could strike out from their island fortress and cross the treacherous waters of Hecate Strait, which they alone had mastered, with little fear of retribution from their mainland enemies.

The first archaeological excavation on Haida Gwaii was that of a shell midden near Masset, conducted in 1919 by Harlan I. Smith of the Canadian Museum of Civilization (PLATE 4). He was following up on his earlier work with the Jesup North Pacific Expedition headed by anthropologist Franz Boas. Smith had served as a photographer on that expedition, taking thousands of photographs of coastal villages from Washington State to Alaska. Unfortunately, his wonderful plates do not include Haida Gwaii villages. Another member of the Jesup Expedition, John R. Swanton, the principal ethnographer of the Haida, did do work at Masset and Skidegate, and Smith may have been influenced by the expedition connection with him to undertake archaeological work near Masset. Since precise techniques like radiocarbon dating were not then available, Smith (1919:MS) greatly underestimated the maximum age of the shell middens on Haida Gwaii and in the Prince Rupert area on the mainland where he also dug.

My own archaeological work on Haida Gwaii was an offshoot of excavations in Prince Rupert harbour that began in 1966. Then in 1968, Wilson Duff of the Royal British Columbia Museum encouraged me to investigate observations he had made on Graham Island of shell middens on raised terraces that marked ancient strandlines from times of higher sea levels. The brief excavations I conducted there at Honna River yielded dates in the 3,000 to 4,000 year range and much evidence of burials and utensils roughly equivalent to those of similar date from the Prince Rupert harbour sequence.

That same year, we discovered another midden at Blue Jackets Creek on Masset Inlet on

PLATE 4
The first scientifically documented archaeological excavations on Haida Gwaii were conducted in 1919 at shell middens near Masset. Harlan I. Smith of the Canadian Museum of Civilization attempted to date the most recent occupations by reference to the age of trees growing on the surfaces of the middens and concluded that the majority were from prehistoric times. *Photograph by Harlan I. Smith, July 1919.* CMC 46,683

5

the north coast of Graham Island, which Patricia Severs (1974) later excavated. The artifacts from 3,000 to 5,000 years ago were strikingly different from those found in the Prince Rupert area, but those from about 2,000 years ago showed strong influences from the adjacent mainland. This indicates the beginning of a trading pattern among the Haida and the neighbouring Tsimshian and Tlingit that led to increased sharing of symbols of wealth and materials of exchange, and eventually to closely parallel art styles that were different from those of groups to the south.

Although many water-logged archaeological sites on Haida Gwaii contain wood objects that would document fully the development of Haida art styles, none has been excavated. The excavation of such sites would be very productive, as was demonstrated in water-logged sites several thousand years old in Prince Rupert harbour, from which decorated wooden bowls, boxes, canoe paddles, etc. were successfully recovered and their artistic qualities preserved, using specialized techniques. And few shell midden sites on Haida Gwaii have been excavated, compared to the mainland, partly due to more expensive and difficult logistics of mounting archaeological expeditions there, but also because the Haida themselves have not encouraged such work. All of the old village sites and shell middens contain numerous skeletons, a reminder of "the great dying" that carried off most of their population in the last century. This has made the Haida particularly aware of the near-impossibility of conducting archaeological research without disturbing many such burials.

SOCIAL ORGANIZATION

The Haida were divided into two social groups, or moieties, called Raven and Eagle. The Raven moiety was subdivided into twenty-two lineages, or families, and the Eagle moiety into twenty-three; the lineages were not grouped into clans. According to John R. Swanton (1905:66), "in olden times each town was inhabited by one family only," but by historic times, all villages contained representatives of several lineages and most contained members of both moieties. Marriages had to take place between Eagles and Ravens, rather than those who belonged to the same moiety, and children became members of the same moiety as their mother.

Each lineage provided its members with entitlement to a range of economic resources such as fishing spots, hunting or collecting areas, and house sites. Other prerogatives included rights to a wealth of myths and legends, dances, songs and musical compositions. Names were a highly coveted lineage property and were bestowed to mark different stages of people's lives. Names were also given to important material belongings such as fish traps, houses, canoes, feast dishes and even feast spoons. Face painting and tattoo designs were also lineage property, as were all crests, of which Swanton (1905:113–15) lists over seventy.

Each household, whose average size was around thirty to forty people (consisting of about ten closely related nuclear families of a lineage), was headed by a chief. The houses of powerful chiefs were large and could contain up to a hundred individuals, including slaves.

Each lineage also recognized the authority of a chief who could act as a war chief in times of conflict. The town chief was the head of the most wealthy or populous lineage in a village, but changed from time to time in accordance with the general fortunes of the lineage or because of the respect commanded by a certain chief. During the last century, for instance, there was intense rivalry between Chief Ninsingwas and Chief Skidegate. According to Newton H. Chittenden (1884:81), a surveyor for the British Columbia provincial government, "They quarrelled bitterly over their rank for a long time, Ning-Ging-Wash, by means of his more liberal potlatches finally prevailing, but not until two of their adherents had been killed."

Chiefly rank was passed down by inheritance through the matrilineal line, usually to a chief's oldest sister's son. Inherited positions determined the order in which chiefs or people of high rank were seated at potlatches and feasts. Those who had not had potlatches given for them, or who did not own houses or major property, were considered commoners. The Haida also owned slaves, who were war captives or the children of captives, often taken from neighbouring tribes on Vancouver Island or the mainland.

The potlatch was the most important Haida ceremony and accompanied the progress of high-ranking people through the social order to mark the giving of names, marriages and deaths. Years of preparation were required to amass the food to feed invited guests and the wealth to distribute gifts to pay for the witnessing of events. The building of a house and the raising of a frontal pole usually called for the major potlatch any chief would give in his life-time.

MYTHOLOGY AND CRESTS

The mythology of the Haida, like that of other tribes on the central and northern coast, is based on the epic cycle of stories about the Raven and his various exploits. The Raven is truly a trickster who liberates humankind from a clamshell, then in one story sets the universe in order, only to threaten it with chaos in the next. The Raven is the most greedy, mischievous and lecherous creature imaginable, but almost without meaning to, teaches humans the arts of living a good life. Haida artist Charles Edenshaw alone could recount several hundred different Raven stories from memory.

One of the best-known of these stories tells how the Raven disguised himself in order to enter the house of the Sky Chief, from whom he stole the sun, moon and stars to give to humankind. In another popular tale, the Raven was hungry, so decided to swim underwater to eat the bait off the hooks of some halibut fishermen. However, the hook lodged solidly in his beak. The fishermen banded together to haul up what they thought was a huge halibut, but got the Raven's beak instead.

Many stories describe the Raven's encounters with supernatural beings and how he acquired other useful things for humans from them, such as fresh water, salmon, the fish weir and the house—the latter from the Beaver.

Most Haida objects are decorated with crests—figures of animals, birds, sea creatures and mythic beings—that immediately identify the moiety (Raven or Eagle) and often the lineage of the owner. On a more subtle level, the placement of a crest figure, and especially the smaller figures attached to its ears, chest or mouth, refers to a specific myth involving that crest. An example is the Edenshaw family's frequent use of the Butterfly on the chest of the Raven, which refers to a series of myths in which the Butterfly is the Raven's travelling companion in the Masset series of stories (Swan 1883:MS, Aug. 10). In the Skidegate series of myths (Swanton 1905A), however, it is the Eagle who accompanies the Raven on his travels. Details such as these make it difficult to read the full range of meaning on a totem pole without a thorough knowledge of the mythology, but there is no one alive today who is familiar with the thousands of myths that have been recorded in various museum archives. Hence, the "text" that can be associated with a particular pole is similar to a Mayan text, in that only glimpses of meaning are possible.

Around 1900, John R. Swanton worked out a list of crests with information from such knowledgeable Haida artists as Charles Edenshaw of Masset, John Cross and John Robson of Skidegate, and Tom Price of Ninstints. These men all had an intimate working knowledge of the mythology and how crest designs should be used on everything from tattoos to totem poles. Tattoos were put on the thighs, chest, shoulders, forearms, backs of the hands and even all of the joints of the fingers.

Although the Haida have almost seventy crest figures, less than a score are in general use. A few crest figures were used by many lineages, and a larger number were exclusive to a few lineages. The Killer Whale, which is a particularly strong feature of Haida art and myth, is a popular crest. All Raven lineages use forms of the Killer Whale as a crest; one of them, the Raven-Finned Killer Whale, refers to the myth in which the Raven pecked himself out of the body of a Whale through the end of its dorsal fin. Eagle lineages of Ninstints use only the Five-Finned Killer Whale, which links them to specific Killer Whale chiefs whose undersea village was near their own and with whom their mythic ancestors had a profitable experience. The tall dorsal fin of Killer Whale crests that belong to Ravens are always black, while those of Eagles have a diagonal white stripe.

All of the land mammals used as crests, except for the Beaver, belong to the Raven moiety. Some of these crests such as the Mountain Goat, the Wolf and the Grizzly are of animals that do not occur on Haida Gwaii; their use was transferred from Tsimshian chiefs on the mainland. All crests of amphibious creatures such as the Beaver and the Frog are the exclusive prerogative of the Eagle moiety and also originated with the Tsimshian. Sea mammals mostly belong to the Ravens, although many Eagle lineages use the Blackfish as a crest. Fish crests are heavily weighted in favour of the Eagle moiety, who use the Sculpin, Skate, Dogfish, Starfish and Halibut. The Ravens share with them the Dogfish and the Skate.

The Raven moiety does not use the Raven as a crest, but the Eagle moiety does use its namesake frequently, as well as many other bird crests including the Raven, Cormorant, Heron, Hawk and Hummingbird. The only bird crests the Raven moiety uses are the Flicker, Hawk and Horned Owl.

The Haida fashioned for themselves a world of costumes and adornments, tools and structures, with spiritual dimensions appropriate to each. The decorations on the objects they created were statements of social identity, or reminders of rights and prerogatives bestowed on their ancestors by supernatural beings, or of lessons taught to them through mythic encounters with the animals, birds, fish or other beings whose likenesses were embodied in the crests passed down through generations.

The abstract concept of art for art's sake had little meaning for the Haida, but they had exceptionally high standards of craftsmanship and the desire to constantly improve their skills. As inhabitants of an archipelago that lacked many of the prized natural resources available on the mainland   such as mountain sheep or goats, major runs of eulachon fish, mineral pigments, and specialized stones and metals for tools—the Haida began about 2,000 years ago to trade in order to maintain status among their neighbours. What they offered in exchange were products of skilled workmanship, especially their exceptional canoes, but ranging over a great variety of objects such as carved and painted chests, as well as other furnishings appropriate to the potlatch feasts of all the other north coast tribes.

They imported the raw materials that they lacked and processed them into highly refined products that they then exported to other tribes on Vancouver Island and the mainland. Such items included copper shields, silver and copper jewellery (after the late eighteenth century), as well as horn bowls, ladles, spoons, and possibly goat's wool blankets. The Haida excelled in making and engraving copper shields, and examples of their work have been collected from the Tsimshian, Tlingit, Kwakwaka'wakw (or Kwakiutl) and most other peoples of the coast.

From the first days of contact, the Haida tailored their production of art to European and American requirements. Just as the traders catered to the Haida by setting up the shipboard manufacture of iron and copper implements and even items of clothing, the Haida developed art and crafts that appealed to the traders. Most popular were small carvings made of argillite (a soft black stone), items of ivory and silver, as well as a wide variety of wooden and basketry "souvenirs." Literally thousands of such items, collected before the end of the sea otter trade in the 1830s, have turned up in the New England states and the British isles. Numbers of them have found their way into museum collections.

The North Coast Art Style

Many features of what is recognized as the north coast art style are shared by the Haida and their mainland neighbours, the Tsimshian to the east and the Tlingit to the north. This is particularly true of flat designs, which use formlines and ovoids. Primary formlines, which are generally black, outline the parts of each figure. Secondary formlines occur within the primary spaces and are usually red. In rare instances, the two colours are reversed for dra-

matic effect. There is a formal grammar of formlines, in which rules control the thickness of the line and the changes of direction.

A rounded, bulging oval-to-rectangular shape called an ovoid is a feature unique to Northwest Coast art. Ovoids are used to portray a creature's eyes and joints, and sometimes teeth or orifices like nostrils and ears. Small faces are often placed within such ovoids; these refer to the loss of the soul as a prelude to death, for the Haida believe that the soul leaks out of the joints or orifices of the body.

The most common Haida artistic motif is the symmetrical flat design, made up of a complex pattern of components, that represents the Chief of the Undersea World (PLATE 5). This supernatural being is prevalent throughout the Northwest Coast, from the prehistoric levels of the Ozette archaeological site in the State of Washington to the ancient burial chests found in caves in Alaska. One of the favourite designs of the Haida, it is a two-dimensional flat depiction of a being with a small body and an inordinately large, broad head that has a cleft in the forehead. The eyes often contain small creatures ranging from profile heads of salmon to double-profile heads similar in form to the larger head itself. The hands are also oversize, with emphasis on the palms, which in rare cases have separate faces portrayed within them. The arms, which are narrow and tightly folded, often have fins hanging from them. All the joints of the being's body are marked with eyes, heads of salmon or human faces. The overall impression is of undulating black bands that sketch out a broad face teeming with other life forms, which some interpret as souls of humans or other beings temporarily contained within this creature and awaiting rebirth into the world above the sea. George T. Emmons (1907:330), who was the major recorder of Tlingit culture and a collector of Tlingit objects for a number of museums, made the following observation:

> The belief in the mythical being Gonaqadet occurs along the whole coast. He lives in the sea, and brings power and fortune to all who see him. Sometimes he rises out of the water as a beautifully painted house-front inlaid with the much-prized blue and green haliotis-shell [abalone], again as the head of an immense fish or as an elaborately painted war-canoe. In decorative art he is generally represented as a large head with arms, paws, and fins.

Despite the great frequency with which the Haida depicted the Chief of the Undersea World on all types of containers such as food vessels, storage chests, chief's seats and even housefronts, they rarely identified it by name. We know, however, from Swanton's observations (1905:18) on Haida cosmology, that this ubiquitous being is called Konankada (or Gonankadet among the mainland tribes of the north coast). In the most general terms, it is the Master of Souls. Its nature is hinted at in the Haida myth of Master Gambler, whose house is mid-way on the journey to the land of souls, or the realm of Konankada. If those who pause to gamble lose to Master Gambler, more people will soon die in their village. If they win, however, the salmon runs in their village streams will increase. This alternation of souls between human and salmon forms one of the central equations of north coast art. The

PLATE 5

A red cedar bentwood Haida storage chest carved and painted with the protective image of Konankada, Chief of the Undersea World. *Collected at the Nass River in 1905 by W. A. Newcombe.* CMC VII-C-109 (s94-6802)

paradigm into which this and many other equations fit is the recycling of souls between human and animal (most frequently salmon) from one generation to another.

Flat Design

Elaborate two-dimensional designs called "flat designs" are characteristic of Northwest Coast art and are tightly controlled by formal canons of both line and form. The Haida made far fewer large-scale paintings, such as housefronts and screens, than their Tsimshian neighbours. The Haida were, however, the masters of subtly sculpted flat design—a kind of bas-relief—in which the secondary and tertiary spaces were enhanced with gently swelling or concave planes between the primary formlines. In the past, the Haida used less complex textured zones of cross-hatching or parallel lines around eye forms than did Tsimshian and Heiltsuk artists. Although early Haida artists are not known by name, art historian Bill Holm (1981:199), after a close study of disparate works such as totem poles, housefront paintings, chief's seats and argillite carvings, identified one early master painter and sculptor as "the Master of the Chicago Settee," after the first piece of his work to attract the appreciation of experts like Holm, Wilson Duff and Haida artist Bill Reid.

From the 1870s on, numerous Haida artists who are known by name became remarkably free and innovative in their paintings, depicting animal, fish and bird forms with a greater degree of realism than before, and often in quite a narrative dimension. This creative development is undoubtedly related to the fact that these artists, of which there were several dozen, were working in both argillite and paint, using formline designs on a variety of objects intended to appeal to foreign visitors.

The best known of these artists were Charles Edenshaw, Tom Price, John Robson and John Cross, but there were many others. A small number of Skidegate artists also applied radical painting styles to box or drum designs with intriguing results. It is virtually impossible to differentiate the nineteenth-century boxes decorated in the various villages of the north coast groups, as these served as containers of trade items among those communities. However, tribal styles are distinctive in boxes and chests owned by chiefs for storing wealth items and for burial chests (or coffins).

John Cross, John Robson, Tom Price and Charles Edenshaw also produced many flat designs that fit into the category of "ledger drawings," a form common to Indian art of the late nineteenth century. These were often elaborate drawings based on tattoo designs, done from memory in ledgers or copybooks provided by the administrators and missionaries who entered Indian communities to educate and Christianize them. Drawing skills were considered important and were encouraged by supplying coloured pencils, crayons and paper. The Haida needed little encouragement in adopting these new materials to provide samplers of totemic and other designs that were much in demand by collectors.

Haida flat design has survived and is in fact thriving in the limited edition print market that sprang up in the late 1960s. Many artists like Don Yeomans, Gerry Marks and Reg

Davidson have produced hundreds of images that are sold in fine art galleries throughout the world. The current master of this form of painting and printmaking is Robert Davidson (a descendant of Charles Edenshaw), whose work is featured in more detail in the final chapter.

Sculpture

Haida sculptures range from 20-metre (65-foot) tall totem poles to the equally complex carved handles of horn spoons. This ability to express artistic concepts over a range of sizes and forms has attracted the admiration of art aficionados worldwide over the past two centuries.

The earliest known Haida sculptures are from cave sites or remote graves of shaman that date from the mid-eighteenth century. The oldest carved poles are undoubtedly shaman grave posts, some of which are late eighteenth and early nineteenth century. They portray primarily human figures, whereas the monumental poles standing in the villages display crests and supernatural beings from mythology. The earliest surviving poles include triple mortuary posts circa 1830 from Kiusta (MacDonald 1983:259) and a large house frontal pole circa 1840 from Hiellan village (PLATE 140) (MacDonald 1983:236). On these four poles, the figures are very large and few in number, with many small faces appearing at the joints, eyes and ears.

The oldest burial chest is from the Gust Island burial cave (MacDonald and Cybulski 1973:26), while a slightly later example from an eighteenth-century mortuary at Kiusta is now in the Royal British Columbia Museum (1321). In both examples, the eye forms are very elongated, with slits in the pupils. Another early piece is a sea lion-shaped bowl (PLATE 25) that is characteristic of the eighteenth-century pieces collected by early explorers.

The majority of Haida carvings created during the last half of the nineteenth century belong to the classic style. Facial features such as eyes, ears, nostrils and lips are very large, and occupy about the same space as the forehead, cheeks and jaw. This gives the animal or bird forms a youthful or even naive look that viewers find appealing. The formal symmetry of the crest art also provides a serenity and charm akin to Egyptian art. Smaller sculptures such as masks and frontlets range from the mystic to the frightening, and occasionally the comical.

Following the tragic depopulation of the late 1860s due to epidemics and the deculturation of the survivors by Indian agents and missionaries in the 1870s and 1880s, the monumental sculptural tradition was abandoned. Carvers miniaturized their production into models of houses and poles, tailoring their art to the tourist market. Few new artists were trained, and eventually the canons and tenets of the distinctive Haida style were lost. The story of the rediscovery of those traditions by the current generation of artists who learned by studying models on dusty museum shelves is told in the final chapter of this book.

CHIEFLY POSSESSIONS

Over time, trade among the people of the north coast groups—the Haida, Tsimshian, Tlingit and Nisga'a—led to the mutual adoption of a limited range of objects and materials that symbolized wealth and prestige. These included the regalia used by chiefs, such as headdresses decorated with ermine skins. Other prestigious objects included artistically decorated chests, boxes and bowls used to store and display the food and wealth that characterized the potlatches.

Chiefs of all the tribes of the north coast possessed an array of regalia, which was documented in drawings by the Russian artist Mikhail Tikanov as early as 1818 and which was compared by travellers and missionaries to robes of the Masonic order with regard to their importance in denoting status. For chiefs, this regalia provided a shared frame of reference for the exchange of wealth between nations with different languages and belief systems.

The full set of chiefly regalia consisted of a Chilkat blanket, leggings, an apron, a frontlet and a pair of Raven rattles (or a drum). A chief was also likely to own a shield-shaped plate of native copper; this was a symbol of wealth that was displayed at feasts and could be exchanged or substituted for other commodities (PLATE 6). After a chief's death, his coppers were often fastened on his memorial pole.

The Haida adopted most of these symbols of chiefly rank, particularly the items of clothing, from the Tsimshian and Nisga'a, and either manufactured their own or acquired them through trade with mainland groups. Very few Chilkat blankets appear to have been woven on Haida Gwaii, however; there was no local supply of goat wool, and the pattern boards from which the blankets were woven are missing from collections from Haida Gwaii, although they are common among the Tlingit. The Haida made their own frontlets and Raven rattles, although on occasion they obtained these items in trade from the mainland.

People of classes other than chiefs, such as shaman or members of secret societies, also had their own particular regalia.

PLATE 6

The chief whose name means Highest Peak in a Mountain Range stands in front of House Where People Always Want To Go at Haina village. This photograph shows a Haida chief of the previous century in traditional dress, displaying his wealth of coppers before his lineage house. *Photograph by Richard Maynard, 1888.*

Clothing

In precontact times, most items of Haida clothing were woven from red or yellow cedar bark. After the bark was peeled in long strips from the trees, the outer layer was split away, and the flexible inner layer was shredded and processed. The resulting felted strips of bark were soft and could be plaited, sewn or woven into a variety of fabrics that were either dense and watertight, or soft and comfortable. Women wore skirts and capes of cedar bark, while men wore long capes of cedar bark into which some mountain goat wool was woven for decorative effect.

Early examples of chief's capes have repetitive patterns of trophy heads, but after warfare was suppressed by the traders, the trophy heads were replaced with crest figures, and the amount of wool used was increased to the point where the cedar bark warps could not even be seen. The fur of sea otter or other animals was added to the neckline of capes for those of chiefly rank.

After contact, the everyday wear of men and women was an unadorned trade blanket, worn as a wraparound garment during the day and used as a covering at night. Slaves were clothed in handed-down blankets.

Chilkat Blankets

Chilkat blankets were the specialty of the Chilkat tribe of the Tlingit, whose territory was at the mouth of the Chilkat River in southeast Alaska. This group refined the style to its highest level in the late nineteenth century, but it had initially been developed among the Tsimshian-speaking people who lived along the Skeena and Nass Rivers on the mainland and had easy access to mountain goats in their hunting territories. Early explorers like Captain James Cook collected cedar bark capes decorated with small amounts of goat's wool; not until the early nineteenth century did full Chilkat-style blankets appear in collections.

Although Chilkat blankets have many design variations (PLATE 7), the most favoured one on those owned by the Haida is a double-profile view of Konankada in the guise of a Killer Whale, flanked by two profile Ravens. This design, according to George T. Emmons (1907:330), is a reference to the first potlatch in the world, which was given by Konankada in honour of the Raven. A vivid description of the first potlatch according to the Tsimshian is provided by Franz Boas (1916:285).

Painted Leather Capes

The Haida were also fond of large elkskin capes with painted panels and fringes on the sides (PLATE 8). The design on these is most frequently that of the Killer Whale, with the Raven, usually in human form, within it. It can thus be equated with the same designs on a Chilkat blanket. The homogeneity of the designs on these capes and their collection provenance sug-

PLATE 7

A Chilkat-style blanket of mountain goat wool and cedar bark. The centre figure, an Eagle, is flanked by two profile Ravens. *Collected from a Kaigani Haida village in Alaska circa 1900 by George T. Emmons.* CMC VII-X-1491 (S91-946)

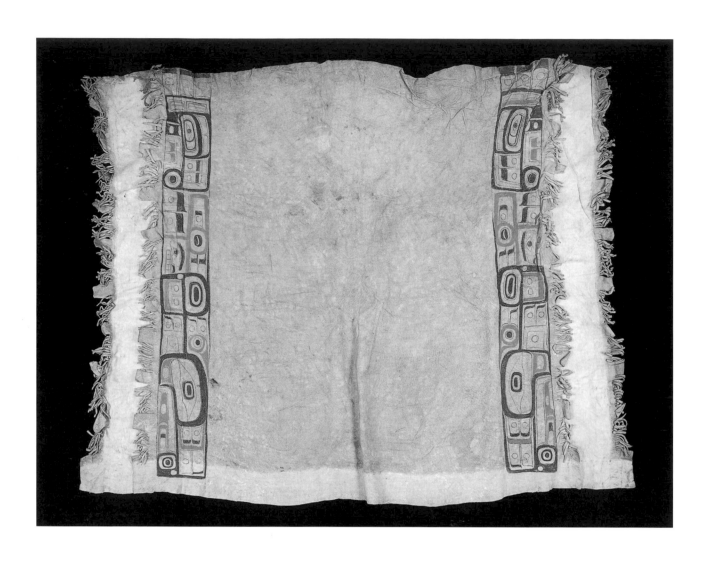

gest they originated among the Kaigani Haida of the Prince of Wales archipelago in Alaska. Many early traders made special efforts to acquire elkskins from the tribes at the mouth of the Columbia River, where elk were abundant, in order to resell them to the Haida.

Tunics, Dance Aprons and Leggings

Another popular item of clothing in the late nineteenth century was a cloth tunic with a single crest on the front and sometimes another crest on the back (PLATE 9). The most prestigious kind was the woven Chilkat tunic, which probably preceded the cloth one. The Chilkat tunic, like the blanket, was a specialty of the Tlingit, and the rare Haida examples were probably obtained in trade. Considerably more common among the Haida were Chilkat woven aprons and leggings, probably also imported from the Tlingit. The design fields on Chilkat tunics, aprons and leggings followed those of the blanket, with slight adaptations because of differences in size and shape.

Clothing worn by chiefs under the Chilkat blanket typically included a dance apron (or wraparound skirt), leggings of leather or cloth, and simple undecorated moccasins. Early aprons were made of tanned deerskin, painted in red and black with elaborate formline designs similar to those on boxes and even housefronts. There is usually a single large Konankada figure, often embellished with human heads in its mouth, but Whale and Raven designs are also common. A few examples, possibly traded from the mainland, are decorated with porcupine quill embroidery. The aprons are fringed at the bottom, a holdover from the ancient skin apron of the shaman. To the fringes are attached deer hooves or brass thimbles to produce a distinctive sound as the wearer moves.

Late in the last century, dance aprons of heavy wool cloth appeared among the Haida but never replaced leather aprons to the same degree as they did among mainland peoples. The decoration consists of a single family crest, cut from red cloth and appliquéd onto the dark blue apron.

Leggings are decorated in much the same way as dance aprons. Early leggings were made of leather, with complex figures painted on them and quill embroidery. After contact, cloth leggings with appliquéd crest figures became popular. The Haida often added puffin beaks or deer hooves as janglers.

Button Blankets

The button blanket, which came into use after contact, has now become the most popular piece of contemporary feast attire. At first, crest designs decorated with dentalium shells were sewn onto wool blankets acquired from maritime fur traders and later the Hudson's Bay Company (PLATE 10). By the middle of the last century, the favoured blanket was made of blue duffle, with the designs appliquéd in red stroud (PLATE 11). Squares of abalone shell were sewn to the eyes and joints of the crest figures to reflect bits of light as the wearer

PLATE 8

An elkskin cape painted with a Killer Whale design on the borders. Such capes were especially popular among the Kaigani Haida and commonly bore this identical design, perhaps symbolizing an honorary rank like captain of a war canoe. *Probably acquired circa 1900 by George T. Emmons for the Lord Bossom collection.* CMC VII-X-783 (S94-6729)

PLATE 9

The bold design of a Mountain Goat crest on a clan tunic of red and dark blue wool trade cloth, adorned with pieces of abalone shell. *Probably acquired at Kasaan village in Alaska circa 1900 by George T. Emmons for the Lord Bossom collection.* CMC VII-X-1078 (S94-6740)

PLATE 10

A trade wool blanket decorated with a human figure outlined by dentalium shells, pieces of abalone shell and trade buttons. *Probably acquired at Kasaan village in Alaska circa 1900 by George T. Emmons for the Lord Bossom collection.* CMC VII-B-1525 (S92-4307)

PLATE 11

A dark blue trade wool blanket with the design of a double-headed Eagle appliquéd on it in red. Trimmed with dentalium shells, ovoid pieces of abalone shell and a border of mother-of-pearl buttons. *Lord Bossom collection, circa 1900.* CMC VII-B-1521 (S92-4306)

danced around a fire. When pearl buttons obtained from fur traders came into use, they proliferated onto the formlines. Today, buttons are sometimes used to fill entire zones of the design elements and even the whole field of the background.

A modern potlatch can bring forward a hundred or more button blankets from the participants. At a traditional naming ceremony, it is now considered essential to present the recipient with a special blanket decorated with a family crest. A century after the button blanket was first developed, it has become a symbol of social and artistic rebirth among the Haida. One Kaigani Haida artist, Dorothy Grant, has initiated a fashion house specializing in appliquéd clothing that she labels "Feastwear" (PLATE 12).

Headdresses

Headdresses worn by chiefs included carved frontlets and painted hats. The item of chiefly regalia that had the most prestige and recognition among the northern tribes was the frontlet, a carved wooden plaque worn on the forehead. The frontlet plaque was carved of yellow cedar, birch or maple, in bas-relief, affixed to a cap that was edged with stiff sea lion whiskers and that had a train of ermineskin. This headdress appears to have originated with the Nisga'a and been adopted into the chiefly regalia of other tribes. The train of densely packed ermineskins may be conceptually linked to Konankada, who is sometimes depicted as a painted housefront surrounded by white clouds or flocks of seagulls that signal the beginning of eulachon runs on the Nass River. The Whale tail of Konankada is always attached to the back of this type of headdress.

Frontlets

All the north coast groups adopted the frontlet, but they each developed distinctive styles. The typical Tsimshian frontlet is a human figure with a head larger than its body and limbs, squeezed into a rectangular or dome-topped plaque that is surrounded by small human or crest animal figures. The frontlet of the Nisga'a of the Nass River has shallow rounded carving of the central human figure with squares of abalone shell surrounding it. The Tlingit frontlet has a more irregular pattern of small figures around the central figure, which is usually a crest animal rather than a human; the colours are more variable than the standard black and red used by the Haida, with a preference for green and grey.

The Haida frontlet is mid-way between those of the Tsimshian and Tlingit, in that animal figures are common in the centre but human figures are not rare. The Haida carve the central figure in higher relief and outline its eyes with a black line (PLATE 13) that among the Tsimshian is rendered by a change in sculptural plane between the eyelid and the eye. Haida frontlet plaques are round or oval as often as they are rectangular. One classic Haida frontlet uses a rectangular frame with a high relief figure of Dogfish Woman (PLATE 14).

The north coast frontlet embodies a complex cosmological message in which the domi-

PLATE 12

A button blanket by Dorothy Grant, Kaigani Haida, depicting the Raven bringing light to the world. This piece was commissioned by Dr. Margaret Hess for the Canadian Museum of Civilization on the occasion of the unveiling of a bronze sculpture on the same theme by Robert Davidson at the Museum of Anthropology in Vancouver, 1986. CMC VII-B-1832 (S95-26,944)

PLATE 13 (page 24)

This chief's frontlet representing the Moon is similar to the one worn by John Robson in PLATE 103. The abalone shell inlays on the face and rim of the Moon reflected the firelight, while the flicker feathers served as an invocation to that bird to carry the chief's prayers skyward. *Probably acquired at Skidegate before 1899 by James Deans for the A. Aaronson collection.* CMC VII-B-690 (S85-3282)

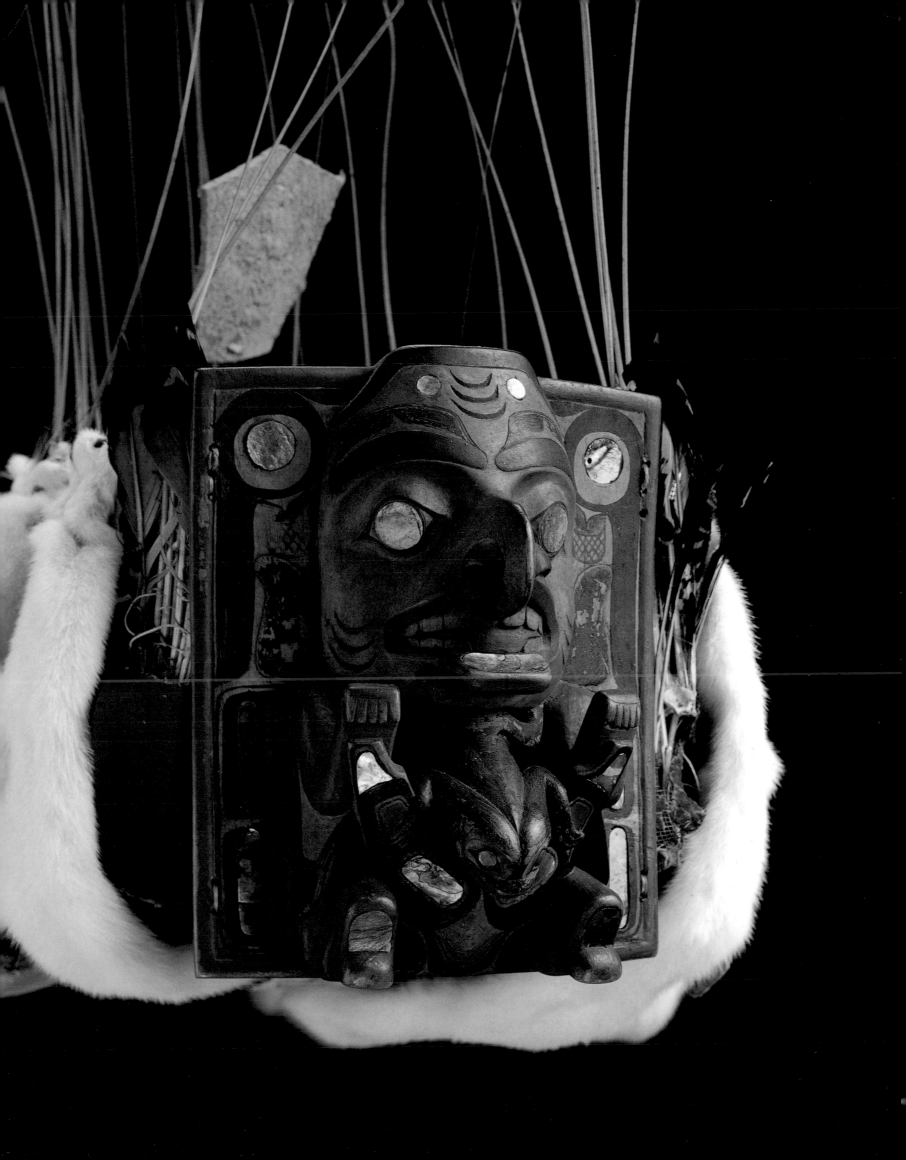

nant reference, conveyed both by the visual forms and by the materials used, relates to beings of the sea and the under world. However, images of humans representing the middle world, and birds the upper world, are not excluded. The sea world and under world references include the painted leather Whale tail that projects from the back and the sea lion whiskers on top that form the cage into which eagle down is placed. The flicker feathers that adorn the sides of the headpiece represent the role of messenger played by these birds, which are said to travel up and down the world tree, or *axis mundi,* and serve as messengers between worlds. Similarly, the ermineskin train refers to the role that creature plays in marking the seasons through its change of colour. The abalone shell, which comes from the sea, is thought to reflect the sky world.

Painted Woven Hats

Early engravings by Russian artists depict north coast chiefs wearing woven hats painted with formline crest designs at the period of first contact. Haida women made these very finely woven spruce root hats that were then painted by male artists with the crests of the commissioning family. Often, the hats had woven basketry rings added to the crown to designate high chiefs. It is claimed that each ring commemorates a potlatch feast the wearer has given, or at least the number of times the owner has been asked to dance at other feasts. Some hats from the north coast have more than twenty such rings.

Haida women excelled in basketry, particularly of spruce root, making not only woven hats but baskets and mats. Their work is different from that of Tsimshian women, who worked mostly with cedar bark strips. This distinction appears to go back at least 2,000 years, to judge from the basketry recovered from Prince Rupert harbour (Inglis 1976).

Both hats and baskets were woven on a stand with a wooden form appropriate to each size and shape (PLATE 15). Designs were either painted on or woven in. The colours of paint were restricted to red and black, with occasional touches of blue or green (PLATE 18). For woven designs, naturally dark-coloured bark was used as a contrast, but plant fibres were also dyed brown, black, red or yellow.

In early historic times, Haida women also sold their baskets and hats to Europeans and Americans who were trading or travelling in Haida territory. Painted woven hats became a popular tourist item late in the last century, and a number of leading Haida artists of the era, such as Tom Price, John Robson and Charles Edenshaw, painted many wonderful examples. Isabella, the wife of Charles Edenshaw, was a very skilled hat weaver and, according to their daughter, Florence Edenshaw Davidson (in Blackman 1982:40), her parents spent many winters producing painted spruce root hats, trays and baskets for sale (PLATE 16). The hats made by the Edenshaws are distinguished by a compasslike design at the top of the crown (PLATE 17).

PLATE 14 (page 25) Although frontlets were acquired from the Nisga'a people, the Haida elaborated the three-dimensional sculptural qualities of the form. This portrayal of the mythic Dogfish Woman is one of the finest examples from Skidegate village. It has a train of ermineskin, flicker feathers at the sides, and sea lion whiskers at the top; the eyes and joints are inset with pieces of abalone shell. *Collected circa 1898 by Charles F. Newcombe.* CMC VII-B-1102 (S92-4298)

PLATE 15 A woman from Masset weaving a basket of spruce root on a stand. Such baskets provided women with an important source of income in the early tourist economy. *Photograph by Edward Dossetter, 1881.* CMC 74-15907

PLATE 16

Shallow trays of tightly woven
spruce root, such as this one
with a Beaver crest, were
suitable for display in a
Victorian home. This one was
created by Isabella and Charles
Edenshaw for sale to travellers,
although it is totally traditional
in style and manufacture.
*Collected at Masset in 1898 by
Charles F. Newcombe.* CMC VII-
B-1135 (S94-6777)

PLATE 17

A woven cedar bark hat, hand
painted with a Frog by Charles
Edenshaw. The four-pointed
star with bicoloured points is
the signature of this artist.
*Collected at Masset in 1911 by
C. C. Perry.* CMC VII-B-899
(S92-4284)

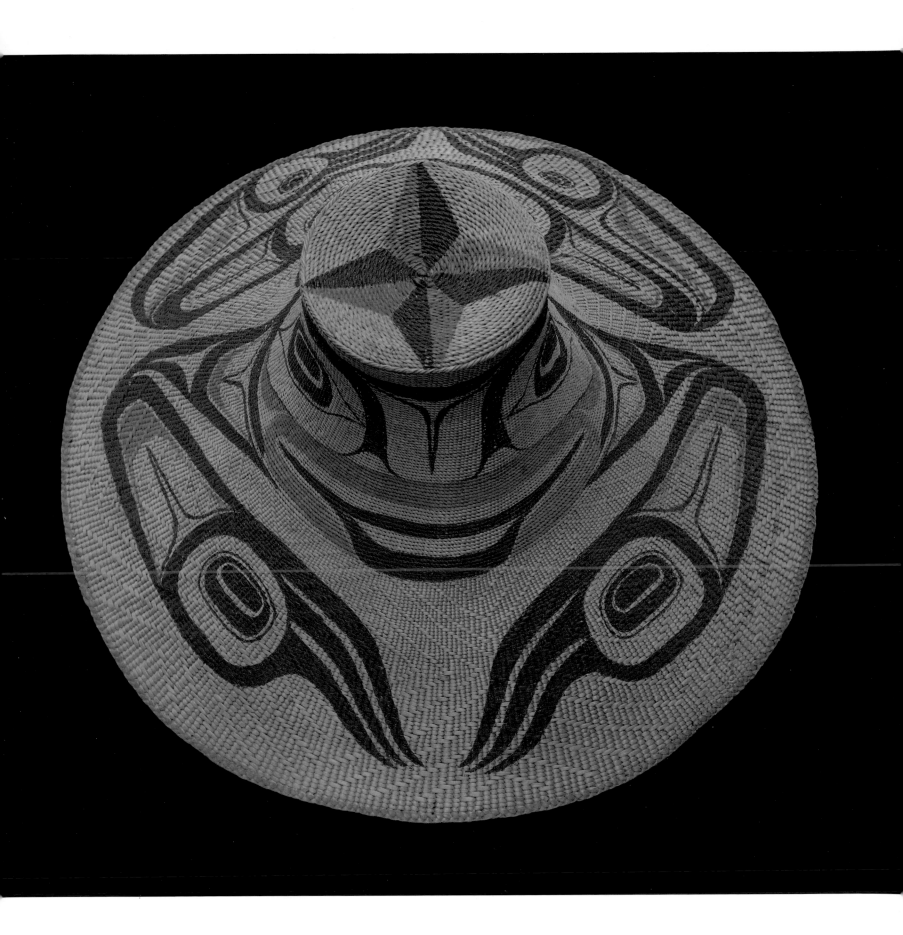

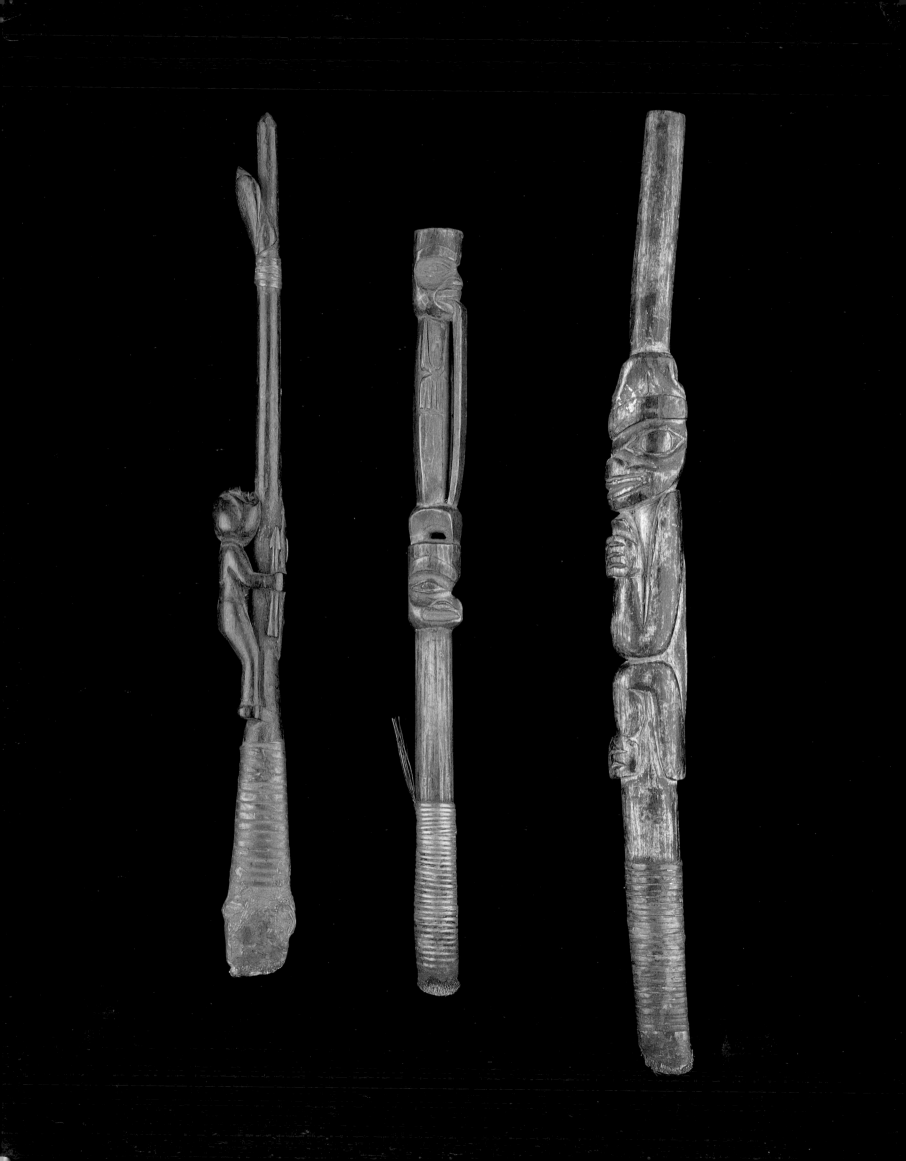

Raven Rattles

Another standard accoutrement of a north coast chief was a pair of Raven rattles (PLATE 19). The basic form is that of the Raven holding a small object in its beak, in reference to the Raven's bringing sunlight to mankind. On the Raven's breast is a flat design image of Konankada. Up to this point of comparison, the symbols are parallel to those of the Chilkat blanket: that is, the image of Raven centred by that of Konankada. The symbolism of the Raven rattle, however, elaborates upon this basic reference to the first potlatch. On the Raven's back is a small human, whose extended tongue is joined to that of a woodpecker type of bird.

Many rattles have a Frog in the place of the woodpecker, and on some, the Raven even holds a Frog in its beak in place of the sun. This may be a mythic reference to the blind Frog People who lived at the mouth of the Nass River and whose plight prompted Raven to steal the sun (Boas 1916:62).

These rattles are complex in their meaning and as yet have not been fully decoded. A possible clue is provided by the Tsimshian myth about the Raven who returns to earth after stealing the sun from the Sky Chief and lands on his back in Prince Rupert harbour (where a large petroglyph marks the spot). The Raven is freed from the rock by a flicker, which uses its sharp tongue to free it. Another Tsimshian myth tells of how the first Raven rattle was brought up on the hook of a fisherman from the Skeena River; from there, its use spread to other people on the north coast. The Haida themselves have no such origin myths and probably received the Raven rattle through prehistoric trade with the mainland.

Raven rattles were usually used in pairs, which associates them with ceremonies elsewhere on the coast to mark the start of salmon runs into the rivers. The swishing noise of the rattles is said to sound like the fins of salmon breaking the surface of the water, which encourages the fish to come past the villages.

Copper Shields

Copper was the ultimate symbol of wealth among the Haida and is associated with Copper Woman of Haida myth. Throughout the coast, shields made of copper were exchanged at ever higher values between chiefs at potlatch feasts. Among the Kwakwaka'wakw (or Kwakiutl) to the south of Haida Gwaii, coppers were particularly associated with the distribution of wealth at wedding feasts. The Haida used coppers as a marker and symbol of wealth, and some wealthy chiefs owned a dozen or more (PLATES 20, 21, 106, 156).

In the Prince Rupert harbour shell middens, the use of copper in the form of bracelets, pendants and tubes can be traced back more than 2,000 years (MacDonald and Inglis 1981:50) and thus appears to be an early feature of north coast trading and warfare. According to tradition, copper came from the territory of the Eyak people in the Copper River area of Alaska, where it occurs with some frequency as pure nuggets in the river gravels.

PLATE 18

Decorated paintbrushes with porcupine hair bristles and traces of pigment, collected from three different villages in 1905 by Charles F. Newcombe. *Left:* The brush from Skidegate is one of the gems of Haida miniature art. It depicts a hunter climbing a tree with his bow and arrow to shoot a bird at the top. CMC VII-B-1022 (s92-4388) *Centre:* The brush from Masset portrays a human figure with an enormous tongue that reaches to its feet. Greatly extended tongues are associated with bears, and the position of the hands pointing downward is also bearlike. The lower figure is the head of a Thunderbird. CMC VII-B-1024 (s92-4388) *Right* The third brush from Kasaan, Alaska, is decorated with the standing figure of a Bear. CMC VII-B-1021 (s92-4388)

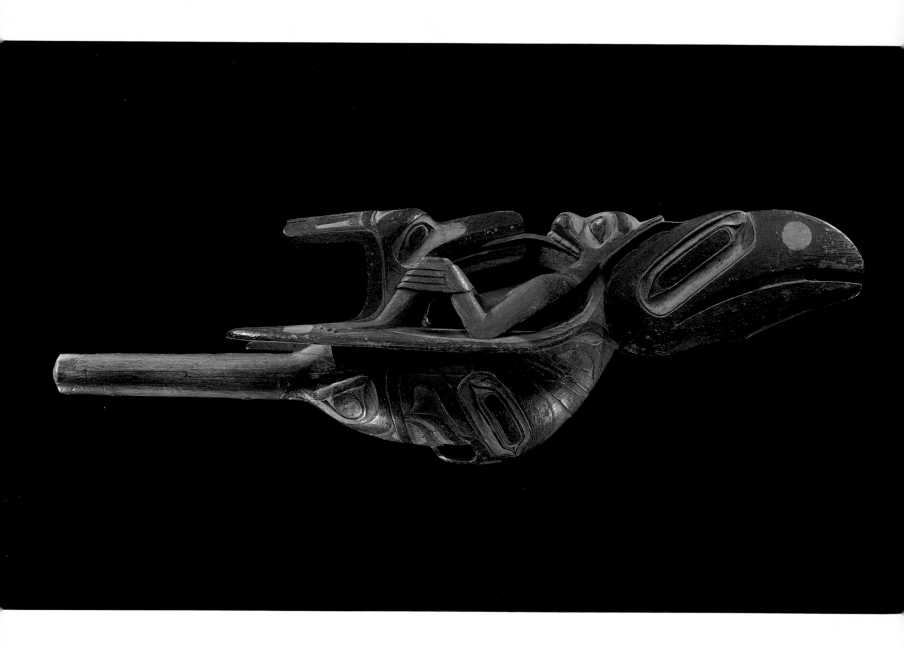

Alexander McKenzie, the Hudson's Bay Company agent at Masset, recorded the following information, which he elicited from local chiefs (1891:12):

> The original coppers were brought from the northern portion of Alaska, and the tradition is . . . that they were first made out of lumps of native copper which were found in the bed of a river there, but latterly the Indians bought sheet copper from the Russians at Sitka, and also in Victoria, and several natives along the coast commenced manufacturing spurious coppers from this material, which ultimately produced a fall in the value of coppers, and by glutting the market destroyed the romance of the idea that the copper was one of the earthliest rarest and choicest treasures fit only to be purchased by great chiefs.

McKenzie also notes that, among the Haida, each copper had its own name. He records the history of a copper called Taow-kee-ass, which belonged to Albert Edward Edenshaw; it was sold to a Tsimshian chief for eight slaves, one large cedar canoe, one hundred elkskins and eighty boxes of eulachon grease.

A number of studies have tried to unwrap the cosmological meaning of the copper shield with varying success. On one level, it represents the ancestors of the owner, and the raised T-shaped bar that divides it is the backbone or skeleton of the ancestors. McKenzie (1891:11) also comments on this feature of the copper:

> A conspicuous mark was always on these, the (T) cross, and on the skill with which this was executed depended in a great measure the value of the copper: This T or indentation is called in Haida *taow-tsoe-h*, namely, "back bone of the *taow*." It was fashioned by hammering on a wooden pattern by a particular process known only to skilful workers, with the result that when the *taow* was finished, the indentation of the T was the same thickness as the rest of the copper plate. If the T proved thinner, the value was considerably diminished; in fact, the copper was considered not genuine.

The portion above the T-bar is often bulbous and represents the head of the ancestor/crest, although among the Haida the rest of the body of the crest is often incorporated above the T-bar. The Haida engraved the design deeply into this upper portion and frequently chiselled out the background to provide a higher relief.

Very small coppers were sewn in numbers onto dance aprons and skirts, and the shape of the copper shield was often used for other objects of wealth such as abalone earrings. Neck-rings made of copper were popular, and copper figurines of humans were also fairly common, but there are no indications as to their use. They invariably have large heads, sometimes with pierced facial features, and even wear small copper armbands. It is possible they were used in curing rites or by shaman at first salmon ceremonies. Much rarer were copper masks (PLATE 22), though similar ones are frequent among the Tlingit.

PLATE 19

Raven rattles such as this one were used by a chief in ceremonies. The different sounds and rhythms produced by a pair of such rattles enhanced the drama of his oratory. On this rattle, the Raven supports a shaman initiate who is drawing inspiration and knowledge from the animal world through the link between his tongue and that of a mythical bird. *Collected on Haida Gwaii (probably Skidegate) in 1876 by Lord and Lady Dufferin.* CMC VII-C-2149 (s85-3308)

PLATE 20

This beautifully engraved copper depicting a Sculpin is a classic Haida object. The bulbous top panel displays the crest of the owner, and the well-fashioned T-bar in the lower half represents the backbone of an ancestor. *Acquired from the Kaigani Haida circa 1900 by George T. Emmons for the Lord Bossom collection.* CMC VII-X-1080 (S94-6768)

PLATE 21

A large copper decorated with a double-headed Eagle. The double-headed Eagle is not a traditional Haida crest but was adopted from the Imperial Russian form of this bird introduced by Russian fur traders in Alaska. *Collected from Skedans before 1900 by Charles F. Newcombe.* CMC VII-665 (S92-4244)

34

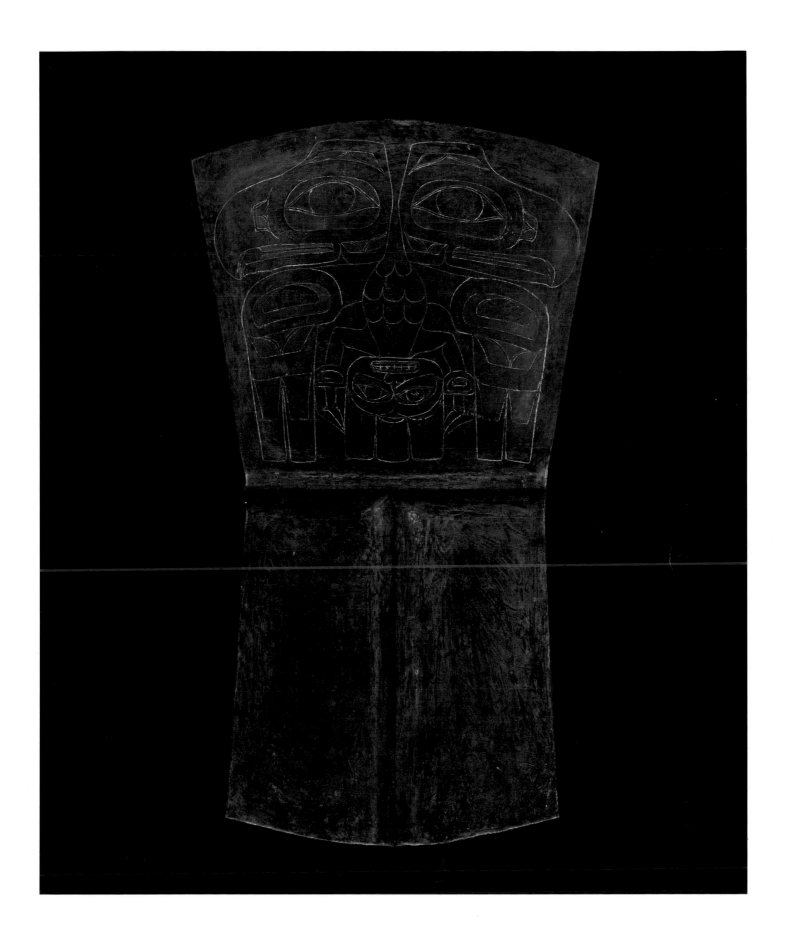

Dishes, bowls, trays, ladles and spoons in a variety of shapes and sizes were part of the expected settings for a feast, and those that were particularly well designed drew much comment from guests. Dishes and bowls were carved out of blocks of wood, moulded out of horn, or constructed by bending boards into a box shape. Bill Holm (1974:31) eloquently captured the essence of these dishes:

> The containers of the northern coast illustrate the remarkable technology of wood and horn working practiced by the native craftsmen. Many different techniques were utilized in making these containers, including carving from solid blocks of wood, shaping carved horn by means of steam, bending planks at steamed kerfs, and fastening joints by pegging or sewing them. The resulting vessels were utilitarian and functional. Their utilitarian roles, however, are over-shadowed by the subtleties of structural form, the richness of surface carving, or the strength of sculptural detail. Function, form, and decoration come together in pieces of aesthetic merit that express the strength and life of a rich culture.

Ladles and Horn Spoons

Ladles and spoons were used to transfer food from serving containers to dishes and to eat with. Ladles were elegantly plain or might have handles embellished with an ancestral figure or a crest design.

Antler spoons with crest figures on the handle appeared on the mainland at the Musqueam northeast site near the mouth of the Fraser River 3,000 years ago (Borden 1982:135), and mountain goat horn cores for spoon handles from 4,000 years ago were found in the Prince Rupert middens. Unfortunately, there are no prehistoric examples of horn spoons from Haida sites, but it is likely that they acquired such spoons very early from mainland groups as part of the intertribal potlatch system.

Individual horn spoons were the most elaborately decorated items at a feast. The bowl of the spoon was made from cream-coloured mountain sheep horn, steamed and bent in a mould. The curved handles were made from black mountain goat horn that provided a field for artistic display second only to that of totem poles. In fact, many spoon handles were faithful replicas of the poles in front of their owners' houses. Some of the most elaborate spoon handles have a dozen or more diminutive figures writhing around and seeming to devour each other on a handle that rarely exceeded 15 cm (6 inches) in length (PLATES 23, 24). Thousands of these exquisite works survive in museums.

Some foods, like soapberries (or Indian ice cream), required special eating utensils. Spoons for eating whipped soapberries were shaped like miniature paddles, which people used to literally shovel the delicacy into their mouths.

PLATE 22

A copper mask, evidently used in rituals since there is a fringe of eagle down glued with pine pitch around the outer edge. This mask was said to have been dug up at an ancient village site at the south end of Masset Inlet and reused in a ceremony at Masset village. *Collected at Masset in 1884 by Israel W. Powell.* CMC VII-B-108 (S92-4185)

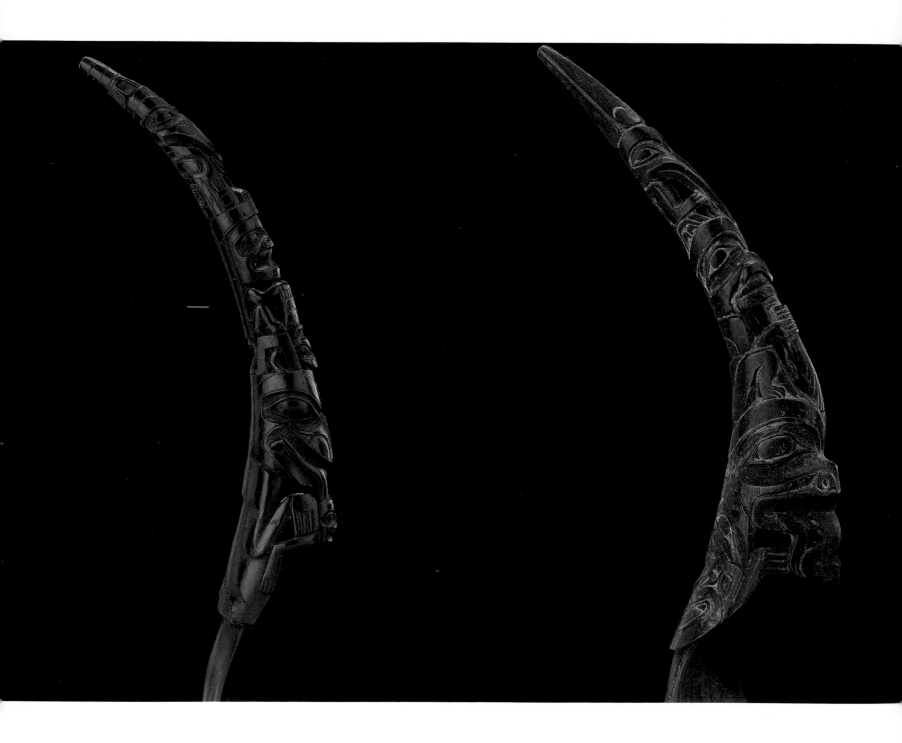

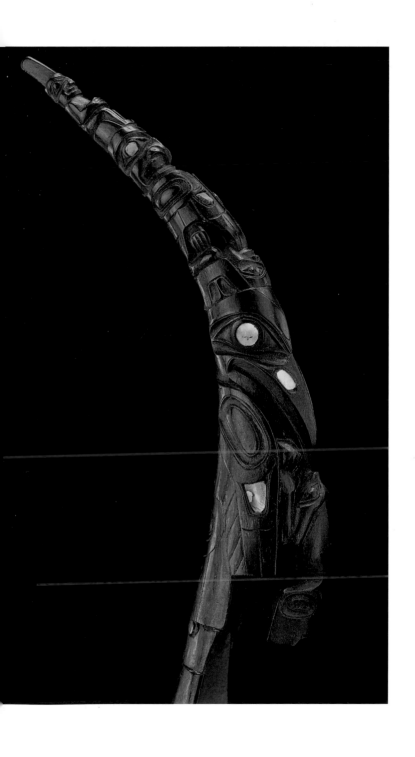

PLATE 23A, B, C

Feast spoons made of mountain goat horn. Each is a miniature version of the same family crests displayed on the totem pole in front of the owner's house.

Left: This spoon handle refers to two well-known Haida myths. The lowest figure represents the story of the hero Nansimget, who is shown grasping the dorsal fin of the Whale that is taking the soul of his dead wife to the undersea world. She is held upside-down in the Whale's large mouth. On top is the Raven holding his beak, in reference to the myth of the halibut fisherman. *Acquired on Haida Gwaii before 1908 for the A. Aaronson collection.* CMC VII-B-719 (S92-4260)

Centre: This spoon handle illustrates the Bear Mother myth. At the base of the handle, the Bear Father attacks the Bear Hunter while his wife and one of their cubs watch from above. The Raven with a raven fin on its head completes the composition. *Collected at Masset before 1894 by Charles F. Newcombe.* CMC VII-B-492 (S92-4221)

Right: On this spoon handle, the Raven holding an otter is the dominant figure on the lower part. Above are two human figures, the first a chief in ceremonial robes, then a shaman with a dorsal fin on his head. Pieces of abalone shell have been set into the handle to make it flash in the firelight. *Collected at Masset before 1901 by Charles F. Newcombe.* CMC VII-B-483 (S92-4212)

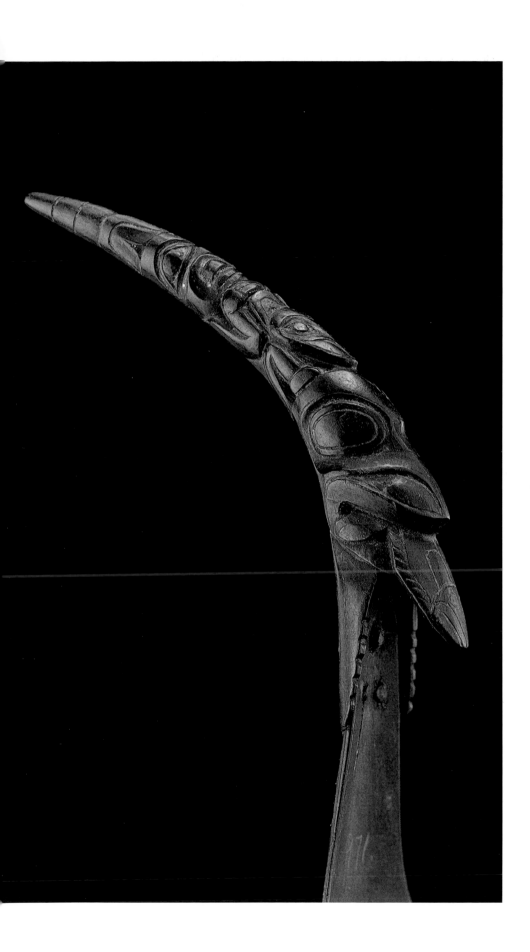

PLATE 24A, 24B, 24C

Feast spoons made of mountain goat horn.

Left: The culture hero Raven perches on a personified rock at the base of the spoon handle. The Killer Whale at the top grasps a drowned human whose soul is being taken to the undersea world. *Collected at Masset before 1901 by Charles F. Newcombe.* CMC VII-B-475 (s92-4209)

Centre: This spoon handle illustrates the Nansimget story. The large Whale at the base is grasping the hero's wife in its mouth while the hero rides its dorsal fin. The Bear completes the composition. Abalone shell inlays enhance the prestige of the owner of this piece. *Collected from the Kaigani Haida before 1901 by Charles F. Newcombe.* CMC VII-B-470 (s92-4204)

Right: At the base of the spoon handle, a large Whale holds a halibut in its mouth. On the Whale's head is the hunter from the Bear Mother story, holding the Bear. *Collected at Masset before 1894 by Charles F. Newcombe.* CMC VII-B-472 (s92-4205)

Food Dishes and Bowls

An individual who possessed a personal or family food dish (PLATE 25) was expected to bring it along to a feast and to use it afterwards to take food home to relatives (Newcombe 1902:MS). The personal food dish, called a *kihle,* is about 30 cm (12 inches) in length, although smaller ones were made for children. A personal "grease" dish was often carved from a solid block of wood, usually alder, which grows on Haida Gwaii, or maple, which was traded in finished form from the Tsimshian. Bill Holm (1974:28) argues convincingly that the prototype for this sort of dish was originally birchbark, with folded and sewn seams at each corner.

Most dishes have decorated ends only, emblazoned with the owner's crest incised in shallow formlines enhanced by red and black paint, though green is sometimes used. The rims often have inlays of shell—operculum, abalone or dentalium—or in historic times, white beads or brass tacks. A significant number also have decorations on the sides, including a broad range of creatures such as Thunderbird, Eagle, Bear, Whale, Beaver and various unidentified mythological beings. The major collector of Haida artifacts, Charles F. Newcombe of Victoria, describes the design of a Thunderbird on a grease dish as follows (1902:MS):

> In these dishes the head occupies nearly all of the surface of the ends. The eyes are the most conspicuous parts and are indicated by the rounded oblong figures on each side with a black center. Above these are the ear symbols, and below the long narrow space with, usually, a curved line above and a straight one below, is the mouth. At the center of the mouth is generally a wedge shaped mark. If complete, this should have its base joined to the upper lip and the point overhanging the lower one. It is more usual to find this V-shaped mark wanting some of its proper characters than to find a perfect one. It indicates the beak of the bird as seen from full front. A few horizontal markings under the mouth are intended to show the foot.

Another kind of dish favoured by the Haida was made of mountain sheep horn that was steamed and bent over a wooden form. The exterior was usually engraved with a complete creature, often a Hawk or Thunderbird. Since sheep horn had to be imported to Haida Gwaii, these are relatively rare in comparison with wooden bowls, and often glow with the patina of long and careful use.

Serving bowls provided by the hosts are the most sculptural of Haida food containers. They are often decorated with human and animal faces and give full expression to the animal forms they emulate (PLATE 26). The most common form of zoomorphic bowl is in the shape of a Seal, often shown holding a small human figure in its mouth or under its chin, a gesture that undoubtedly had some mythical significance. Incised formlines delineate the Seal's joints and front flippers. The seal-shaped dish was used to serve seal oil. Other figures such as the Beaver, Sea Otter or even Dragonfly also decorate serving bowls. The rims of

PLATE 25

This ancient style of carved wooden food bowl, which depicts a Sea Lion in a floating position, is heavily impregnated with grease. The creature's head resembles that of a bear, with prominent ears that are not possessed by sea lions. *Acquired on Haida Gwaii in the early nineteenth century by Philip Henry Hind, later in the James Hooper collection, London.* CMC VII-X-1458 (S94-6747) these vessels are often embellished with opercula shell or sea otter teeth.

Dishes for serving seal or eulachon oil, to judge from their glossy patina, were also frequently made in the shape of canoes. Most are plain, perhaps to emphasize the abstract sculptural form of the canoe, but some have incised designs similar to those painted on actual canoes.

Bentwood Trays and Serving Dishes

A variety of containers for the feast, including trays and serving dishes, were made by the bentwood technique, in which a single plank was kerfed, steamed and bent at three corners, then pegged together at the fourth. Bases were morticed and pegged to the sides.

Shallow rectangular bentwood trays were standard items at a feast. Some large trays for serving smoked or roasted fish were up to 1.5 m (5 feet) in length. The sides were often of alder, and the bottom was generally red cedar. The shape of the top of the rim alternates between concave and convex on each of the four sides. Most trays have a raised flat pedestal at each end, on which to rest spoons.

A deeper version of the bentwood tray is actually a serving dish, ranging from large shallow-sided soup dishes to deep-sided boxes for berries or crabapples in eulachon grease (PLATES 27 to 34). These bentwood dishes were often made in the shape of animals or humans, with faces and hands at one end, and hips, legs and feet at the other. The sides of some dishes bulge out, considerably enhancing their zoomorphic nature, and are usually embellished with two-dimensional bas-relief carving or painting. Some examples position the decorative figures upside-down, but the majority are right-way up. The most elaborate example has a sculptured face and tail on the ends, and bas-relief arms, legs and hip joints on the bulging sides. This type of bentwood dish is often so animated in design and execution that it appears to be alive. Covers made of tightly woven cedar bark were used to keep dirt and insects out of the food (PLATE 27).

PLATE 27

A bentwood food dish with its
cover of woven cedar bark.
The main figure is that of a
Hawk; at the opposite end is
an inverted human figure.
This dish belonged to Chief
Klue of Tanu, who took it
with him when he moved to
Skidegate. *Collected at
Skidigate circa 1900 by Charles
F. Newcombe.* CMC VII-B-740
(S92-4270)

PLATE 28

The isolated decorative elements on this bentwood food dish do not form a coherent design. Such fractured designs seem to have appeared more frequently in the late nineteenth century, perhaps as a result of the disappearance of the traditions that guided the art forms. As well, pieces with such designs were sold mostly to artistically naive travellers. *Collected in 1914 by Thomas Deasey, the Indian agent at Masset.* CMC VII-B-1158 (S94-6748)

PLATE 29

An exquisite example of a deep bentwood food dish of yellow cedar. The complex Whale designs are inlaid with two kinds of shell, opercula and abalone. *Acquired about 1900 for the Lord Bossom collection.* CMC VII-X-1093 (S94-6746)

PLATE 30

A deep bentwood food dish. The design on it, originally painted in black and red, is that of a Whale with Nansimget hanging onto its head. Large feast dishes like this one could hold an entire 22.7-kg (50-pound) roasted salmon. *Collected at Skidegate in 1897 by Charles F. Newcombe.* CMC VII-B-739 (S92-4266)

PLATE 31

A bentwood food dish made about 1850, decorated with brass corner plates. The design depicts a bird, possibly the Thunderbird, with a profile human figure on its back between the wing and tail feathers. The theme of carrying ancestors or mythic heros to the sky or undersea world is a recurrent one. *Collected on Haida Gwaii in 1898 by Charles F. Newcombe.* CMC VII-B-142 (S94-6799)

PLATE 32 (facing page)

A deep bentwood food dish depicting the wings and tail of a bird. An unusual quartered device appears beside the wing joint on the long side. The rim is decorated with opercula shells. *Collected at Masset before 1901 by Charles F. Newcombe.* CMC VII-B-334 (S94-6753)

PLATE 33

A deep bentwood food dish with a bird design. The slightly bulbous sides are incised and painted, with a particularly fine inverted human head over the forehead of the bird. *Collected at Skidegate in 1899 by Charles F. Newcombe.* CMC VII-B-341 (S92-4201)

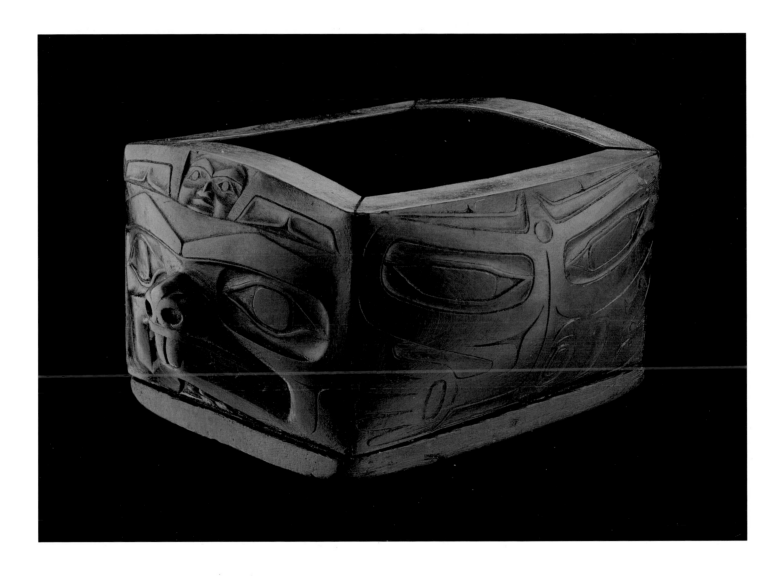

PLATE 34

This fine example of a bentwood food dish portrays a Beaver crest in which a human figure is manifested by hands on the sides and a face between the ears of the Beaver. *Collected at Skidegate in 1886 by Reverend Thomas Crosby.* CMC VII-B-97 (S94-6739)

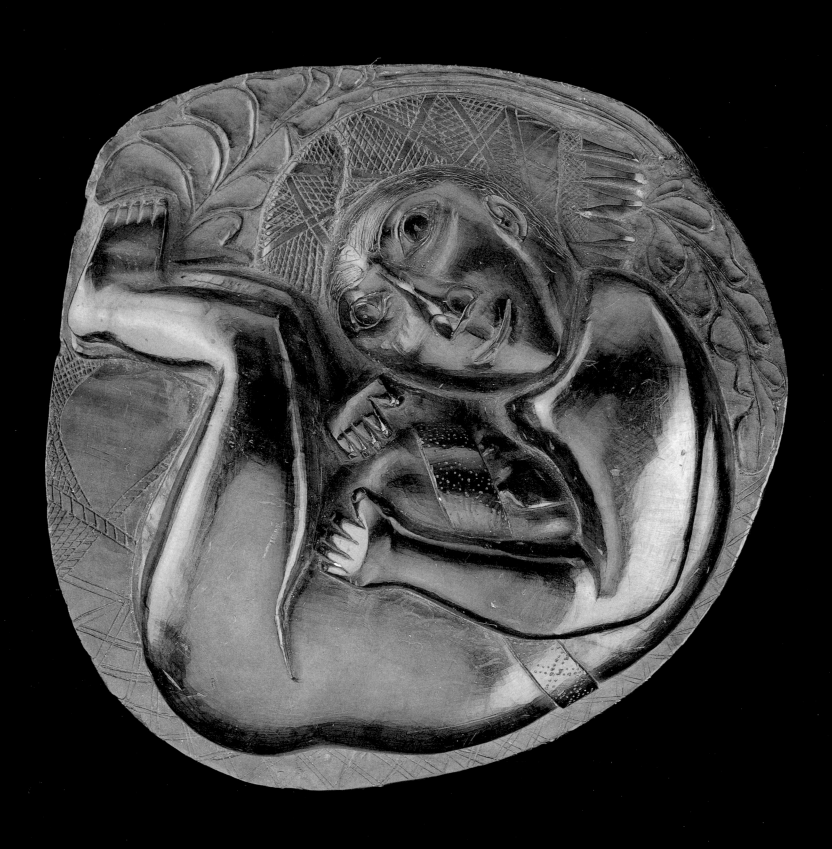

SHAMANISM

The Haida and their neighbours held in common a set of beliefs about the way the human world interacted with the natural and supernatural worlds, though the Haida also had some profound differences in outlook. The shared concepts centred around curing the sick, ensuring the supply of fish and game, and controlling or at least influencing the weather. Among the ranks of shaman were specialists whose powers were particularly effective within a selected range of tasks such as securing the outcome of major enterprises like trading expeditions or warfare.

Both genders could be shaman, but more often it was men who chose the calling. Women shaman focussed more on curing illnesses and the difficulties of childbirth (PLATE 35) and, in rare cases, on power over animals and fish. Although shaman could come from any rank except slaves, they were usually members of high-ranking families, often even the brother of a chief; thus, together they combined both secular and supernatural control at the head of a lineage. John R. Swanton was able to secure detailed information as to how a person became a shaman (1905:38):

> A shaman was one who had power from some supernatural being (*sga'na*) who "possessed" him, or who chose him as the medium through which to make his existence felt in the world of men. When the spirit was present, the shaman's own identity was practically abolished. For the time he was the supernatural being himself. So the shaman must dress as the spirit directed him, and, when the spirit was present, spoke in the latter's own language . . .
>
> The calling of a shaman was generally hereditary in his family, the order being usually from maternal uncle to nephew. Before he died he revealed his spirits to his successor, who might start with a comparatively feeble spirit and acquire stronger and stronger ones. The principal classes of supernatural beings who spoke through shamans were the Canoe-People, the Forest-People, and the Above-People.

Alexander McKenzie (1891:57) also made some observations about shaman in Masset:

> There were no prescribed stages or degrees in the initiation of a medicine-man. (Haida *Sah-gah*). The aspirant to that office was instructed by another medicine-man, generally his uncle,

to whom he succeeded, and on his aptitude to learn the system did the length of his probation depend . . .

. . . Haida doctors never used the drum by way of divination, nor did they employ passes or signs among themselves. Their great aim was to avoid meeting, as they professed to be afraid of each other, and the custom was for each doctor to magnify himself and reduce his rival. They professed to fight in visions.

Much of what we know about shaman is provided by commentary on particular individuals, sometimes by traders, travellers and ethnographers, but mostly by missionaries, although the latter and shaman were mutually suspicious of each other as competitors. The most famous shaman was, without doubt, Dr. Kudé of Masset; numerous photographs taken of him in the 1880s and 1890s show that he fitted the image of a shaman perfectly. Dr. Kudé left his shamanic paraphernalia, including fish effigies he must have used for first salmon ceremonies, to the Pitt Rivers Museum at Oxford University. He appears in a famous photograph of three shaman from Masset dressed in a mixture of sacred and secular clothing (PLATE 138).

The dress of a male shaman is described by Swanton (1905:40):

The dress of a shaman differed somewhat in accordance with the kind of spirit speaking through him. Usually he wore a dancing blanket (Chilkat Blanket), carried an oval rattle, and had a number of bone "head-scratchers" hung around his neck. His hair was allowed to grow long, and was never combed or cleaned. Sometimes he wore a bone stuck through it; at others he wore a cap slanting upon either side to a ridge at the top; sometimes he wore a circular fillet. He always wore a long bone through the septum of his nose.

The traditional clothing of a shaman is particularly well documented in the art of the Haida, who portrayed the shaman on the pair of posts that flanked his or her mortuary to warn off trespassers. The costume depicted is invariably a fringed apron ornamented with deer hooves or puffin beaks. A male shaman always wore his hair long, collected in a bun on top of his head, topped with a wedge-shaped or pointed hat, or a crown of grizzly bear claws. The crown of claws (or occasionally goat horns) is more usual among the Tsimshian but was frequently depicted in Haida argillite portraits of shaman, perhaps because it appealed to tourists (PLATES 36, 37).

Wooden carvings of shaman are often very naturalistic, and a dozen or two were made by Simeon Stiltla, Charles Edenshaw and possibly by others (PLATE 38). New documentation indicates that the works once attributed to Gwaitilth are actually by Simeon Stiltla (1833–1883). The most elaborate of these pieces, such as the one collected by John R. Swanton for the American Museum of Natural History, show the dead shaman laid out, knees bent, in his mortuary house; often he is clutching in one hand a globular rattle with a human or animal face on it, and in the other a soul catcher (PLATE 39).

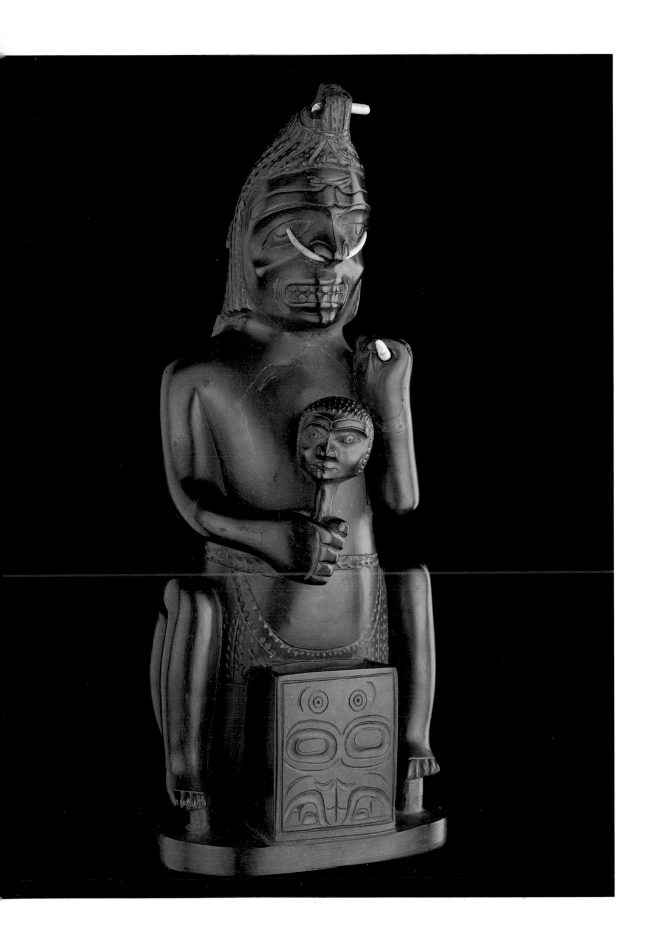

It is said that shaman on the north coast could see the soul departing from a patient's body, as if it were a firefly or small light darting around, and the Haida also seemed to identify the Dragonfly and Butterfly with human souls. The shaman's task was to capture the lost soul in a double-ended soul catcher, then trap it inside with a plug of shredded red cedar bark until it could be blown back into the patient. According to Reverend Charles Harrison (1925:98), "Another familiar of Haida shaman was the killerwhale that was considered to be a bearer for the souls of those who drowned to the realm of the sea chief who was the master of drowned souls."

The shaman wore a neckring of hide over a frame of wood, from which were suspended a dozen or more charms (PLATE 40). Thousands of these charms survive in museum collections, unfortunately without specific documentation. Bird and otter figures are the most common, followed by fish and whales, though many necklaces have only pointed bone pins or bear or beaver teeth attached to them. Rarer shaman charms depict human parts like legs or a hand, or monstrous figures with no natural counterparts. Halibut figures seemed to be a favourite of the shaman, perhaps as art historian Aldona Joanitis (1981) suggests because of the liminal state that halibut fishing, which is done at great depths, represents. Hauling up a 136-kg (300-pound) halibut on a kelp line from a depth of hundreds of metres must have called on supernatural strength more then anything else a Haida fisherman did. McKenzie (1891:59) notes that "To catch eight halibut was a subject for congratulations."

The Haida preferred to obtain their charms from Tsimshian or Nisg̱a'a shaman, who were thought to be especially powerful. The large number of shaman charms that has survived may be due to the fact that they were made of enduring materials like teeth, bone, antler and stone; the Haida often inlaid theirs with small pieces of abalone shell. Also, they were placed in shaman's tombs well away from villages and could be touched only by other shaman.

Haida shaman employed three types of rattles. One is globular in shape and filled with pebbles, or later trade beads, to produce a distinctive sound when shaken in a variety of rhythmic ways appropriate to the purpose of the ceremony. One side of the rattle usually has a human or animal face in full sculptural form, and the other side an engraved and painted flat design of stylized formlines (PLATES 41, 42, 43, 110). Some rattles, however, are sculpted on both sides.

The second type of rattle consists of hoops of wood with crossbars, to which are attached deer hooves or puffin beaks. Deer hooves have been used by shaman in the northern hemisphere since palaeolithic times, and it is claimed that fetal caribou hooves made a sound that was particularly attractive to herds of caribou, which would be lured to approach the shaman and of course his hunter companions.

A third type of rattle, unique to Haida shaman, was the double-headed dance wand hung with puffin beaks (PLATES 44, 45). Puffins were significant because they were diving birds that suddenly disappeared into another cosmic zone beneath the sea. Puffin beaks were also suspended on a circle of wood that represented a cosmic doorway.

PLATE 37A, 37B
Front and rear views of an argillite carving of a shaman with a chief and his slave, which relates to a story about a shaman from Tanu. It was probably carved at Skidegate. *Collected at Carcross, Yukon Territory, in 1972 by Dr. Catherine McClellan.* CMC VII-X-484 (s94-6805 front, s94-6806 back)

PLATE 38

This wooden figure of a shaman has a large Killer Whale fin protruding from his head. The face of the same creature is portrayed on his apron. The symmetrical position of the hands is unusual for a shaman and may indicate that he is diving or swimming in the undersea world of the Killer Whale chief. *Purchased in London, England, in 1976.* CMC VII-B-1654 (S94-6774)

PLATE 39

A model of a shaman's mortuary showing the placement of his body with his head resting on his box of charms. The image of the shaman is repeated on the corner posts, and the large Raven stands guard on the top. Many actual mortuaries like this were placed on small islands near the old villages, but all of them have been looted by curiosity seekers. This fine model was made by Simeon Stiltla in 1900 for John R. Swanton and is now in the American Museum of Natural History.

PLATE 40

A shaman's charm necklace for effecting cures. The fishlike figure at the centre is a "mountain demon" according to James Deans. John R. Swanton (1905:275) identifies this as a *sangu*, or "halibut gills," a crest of the Stastas Eagles lineage. *Acquired on Haida Gwaii in 1899 for the A. Aaronson collection.* CMC VII-B-871 (s92-4280)

PLATE 41

Robins were thought to be familiar spirits of shaman, perhaps because of their migratory behaviour. The wormholes and decay in this shaman's rattle indicate that it was taken from a grave on Haida Gwaii. *Collected at Masset at the turn of the century by Edward Harris, a Hudson's Bay Company fur trader.* CMC VII-X-276 (s94-6776)

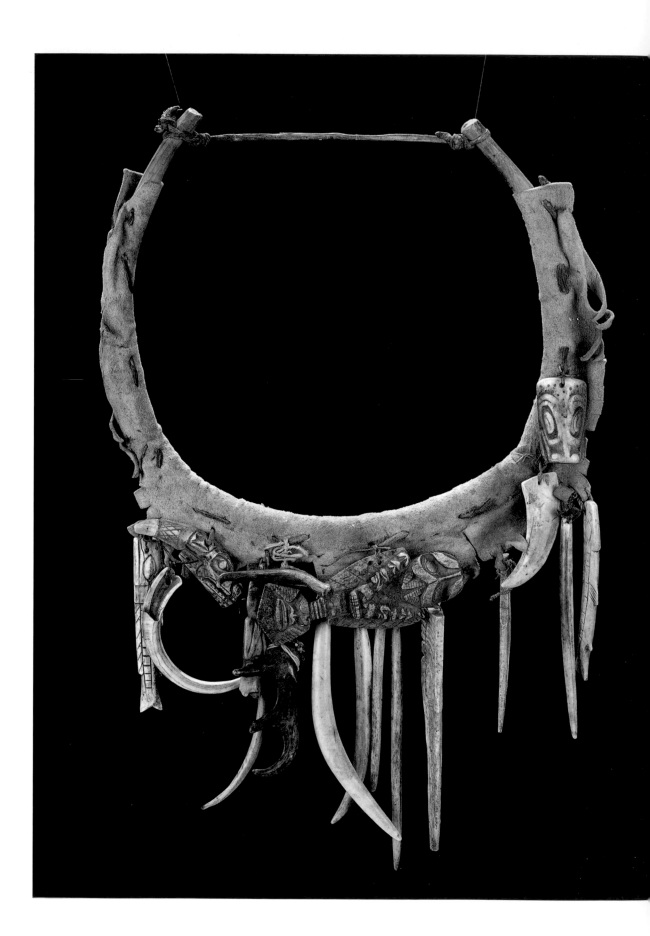

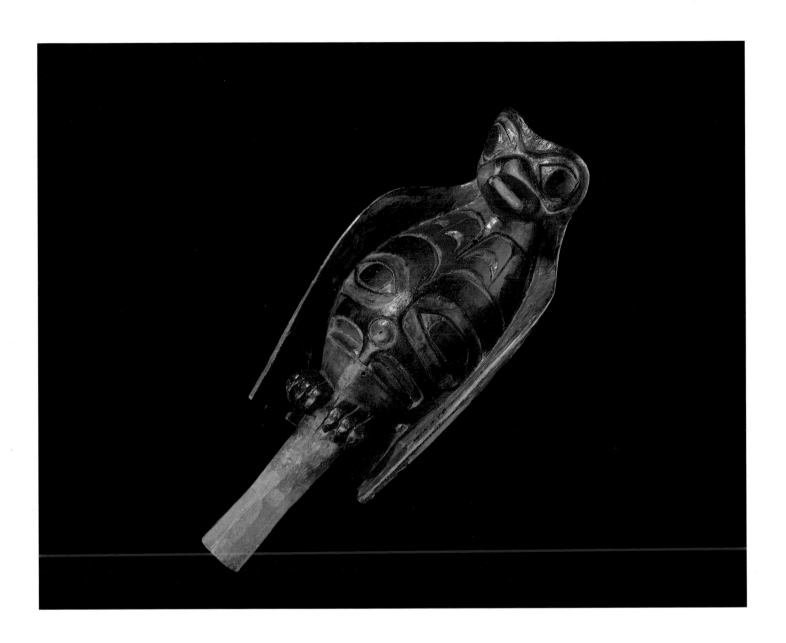

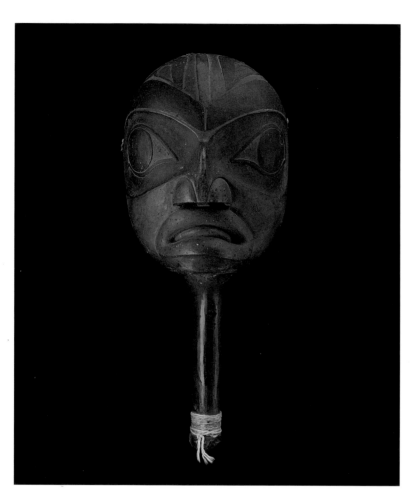 

PLATE 42A, 42B

Front (*left*) and side views of a
shaman's curing rattle, with a
human face sculpted on one
side and a two-dimensional
design of a Sculpin on the
other. *Acquired on Haida Gwaii
in 1899 for the A. Aaronson
collection.* CMC VII-B-672 (SS92-
4249 front, S92-4250 side)

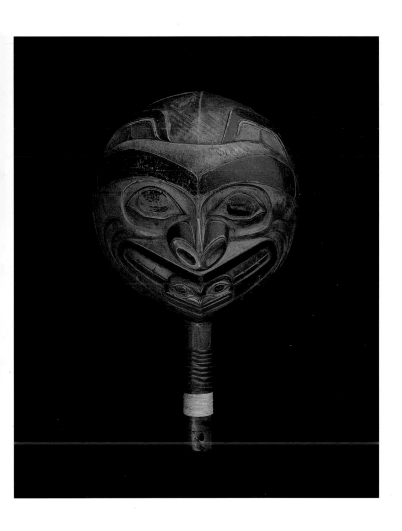
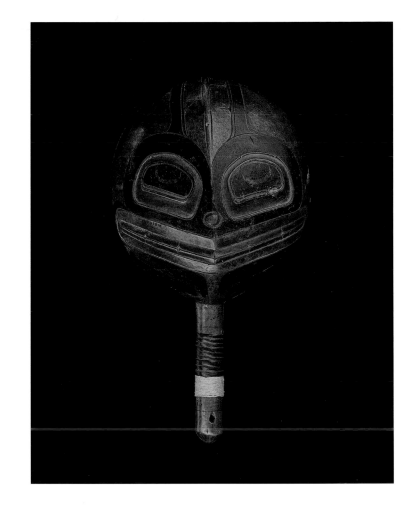

PLATE 43A, 43B

On the front of this shaman's curing rattle (*left*) is a Bear with the head of a Frog in its mouth. The back portrays a Sculpin head. *Collected on Haida Gwaii in 1884 by Alexander McKenzie for Dr. W. F. Tolmie of the Hudson's Bay Company.* CMC VII-B-669 (s92-4247 front, s92-4248 back)

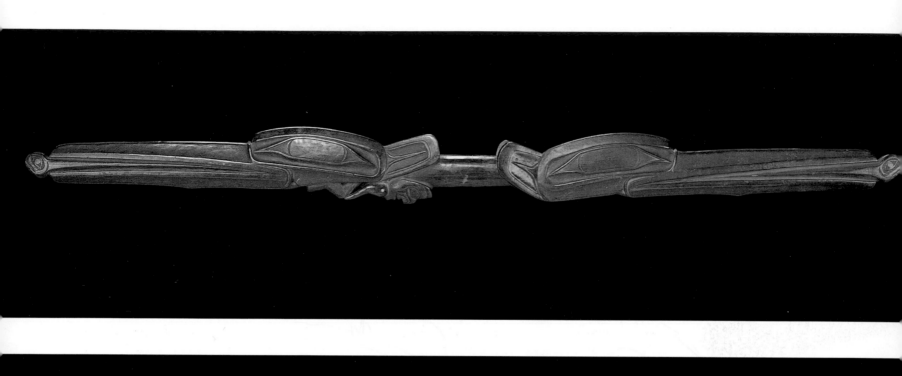

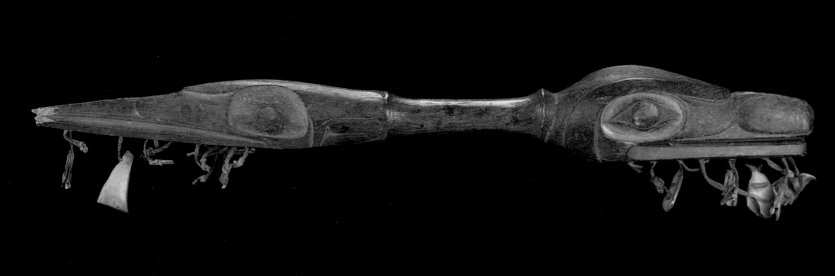

PLATE 44

A shaman's dance wand with
the symmetrical heads of two
Cranes eating some kind of
fish, a variation on the double-
headed pattern of the soul
catcher itself. This very early
piece was probably removed
from a shaman's gravehouse.
*Collected on Haida Gwaii in
1879 by Israel W. Powell.* CMC
VII-B-117 (S92-4189)

PLATE 45

This shaman's dance wand has
puffin beak rattles attached to
it. One end depicts a Crane's
head and the other end a Sea
Lion's head. *Possibly acquired
by James Deans before 1899 for
the A. Aaronson collection.* CMC
VII-B-686 (S92-4252)

PLATE 46

A red cedar bentwood box
used to hold a shaman's
charms. The highly stylized
design includes a bird's head
on one side. The wear and
grease on the box indicate long
service. *Probably removed from
a shaman's grave on Haida
Gwaii before 1899 by James
Deans for the A. Aaronson
collection.* CMC VII-B-726 (S94-
6800)

The shaman kept his paraphernalia in a special box that was distinctive in form and decoration. It was stoutly made to serve the shaman for his lifetime and bore protective animal images (PLATE 46). In it, he kept his soul catcher, charms, rattles and, in some larger boxes, a set of masks. According to Franz Boas (in Swanton 1905:43), Haida shaman do not wear masks, though Tlingit shaman do. However, there is some evidence that Haida shaman did wear masks on rare occasions (PLATE 47).

Objects and motifs associated with shamanism were not appropriate for trade; they were custom made for individual shaman and buried with them. Consequently, the range of motifs and styles associated with shamanism are archaic in many respects. There is a heavy emphasis in shamanic artifacts on Killer Whale motifs or creatures from the liminal space of the intertidal zone, like octopus, or the depths of the ocean, like halibut.

SECRET SOCIETIES

Secular power in Haida society was wielded by the chiefs, who, unlike their Kwakwaka'wakw (or Kwakiutl) neighbours to the south, never yielded their power each winter to the heads of the secret societies. Nevertheless, by the mid-eighteenth century, the Haida began to practise much weaker forms of secret society winter dances, which they learned from captives taken in wars against the Heiltsuk in particular. However, as many of the captives were of low rank and had not been fully initiated into secret societies, the Haida were copying poorly understood models. Like the Tsimshian, the Haida were late recipients of these winter dance societies and never elaborated them further. Photographer Edward Curtis (1916:130) noted that the Haida knew little of the underlying myths or esoteric features of the winter dances, though they did preserve the names of a dozen different kinds and performed them at all winter festivities, including those to mark the raising of a totem pole or the building of a house.

The Tsimshian have a well-known story about how secret societies were acquired by two brothers out fishing (Boas 1916:285). The Haida version is different: according to it, secret societies were stolen by one of their own supernatural beings, Qingi, who travelled from Haida Gwaii in a small black canoe called Tobacco Canoe to the house of the Chief of the Undersea World. One part of the long story illuminates some features of Haida dance hats (Swanton 1905:157):

> Qi'ngi sat by himself on one side of the house, and at intervals opened his bag, took out a piece of dried salmon, and ate it. For this all of the supernatural beings laughed at him. Then he put on a tall dance-hat and began to dance. At once they heard the "spirits" (secret-society whistles), —the first time that human beings had heard them. These whistling sounds were caused by flickers. Qi'ngi's hat now began to grow; and as it grew, sea-gulls and cormorants flew from the joints, and scattered their excrement over everybody, so that the supernatural beings covered up their faces. By and by his hat shrank again, and he took it off.

PLATE 47

A shaman's mask of red cedar trimmed with eagle down. The crown of grizzly claws was copied from Tsimshian shaman. Masks were only very rarely used by Haida shaman, so this one was probably made for sale to visitors. *Collected on Haida Gwaii by Israel W. Powell in 1879.* CMC VII-B-11 (S92-4165)

PLATE 48

A wooden Killer Whale dorsal
fin ornament with streamers of
human hair. As many as five
similar fins were tied to dance
cloaks, or a single one was tied
to the head of a dancer. From
a donated collection, no
specific acquisition
information. CMC VII-X-31
(S94-6783)

PLATE 49 (facing page)
A dancing spear that belonged
to the Warrior Society. The
alternating thick and thin
spiral lines imitate patterns
observed on the legs of tables
and chairs aboard European
ships. *Collected on Haida
Gwaii in 1879* by *Israel W.
Powell.* CMC VII-B-129.2
(S4192.2)

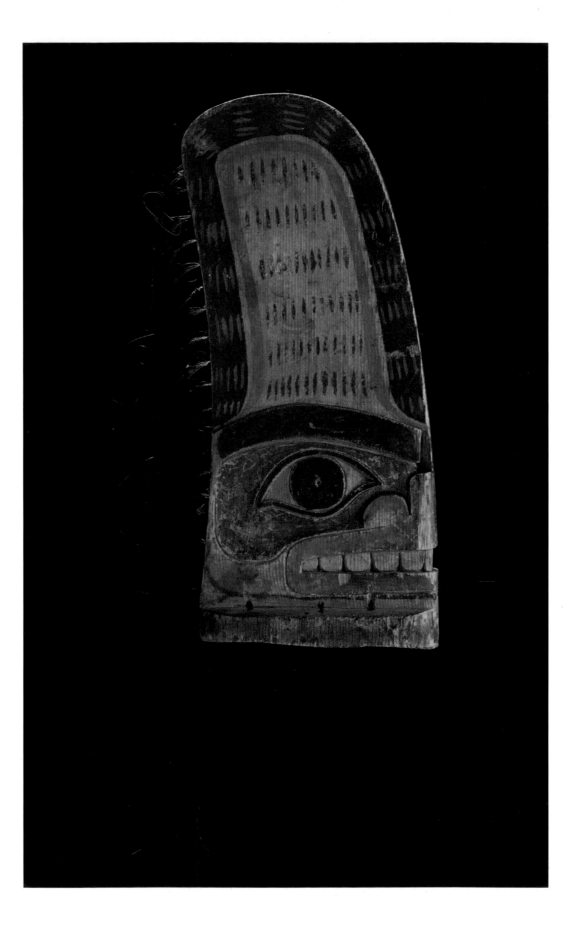

The living beings flying out from the joints of the stack of rings on the dance hat are a revealing reference to the Haida belief that the rings represent the spinal column of supernatural beings and are a source of new emerging life. The story ends with Qingi escaping with the new dances he had seen to introduce them to the Haida.

Among the Haida, the winter dances began to die out in the mid-1870s, although they were held sporadically for another decade. There are, consequently, few eyewitness accounts of the performances. Nevertheless, Curtis (1916:142–43) was able to find Haida who still vividly recalled such events from their childhood:

> Little children could be initiated into the society . . . They spent the eleven days behind the curtain, supposedly dead for eight days and absent with the spirits for the remaining three, and when the dancing began they came out and stood in front of the curtain . . .
>
> After retiring behind the curtain the elder initiates also remained in concealment for eleven days, except that in the evenings of the first eight days they came out in full paraphernalia and went with characteristic actions through the village. During the day they too were supposedly lying dead behind the curtain.
>
> At the end of eight days many whistles sounded in the woods, and gradually receded, and it was said that the spirits of the initiates were being carried away by supernatural beings. For the next three days the initiates remained in constant hiding. Then on the twelfth morning those initiates who were to represent dancers appeared on the beach as if they were wild creatures just come out of the woods after their absence with the supernatural beings. The members of the fraternity proceeded in a body to catch them with ropes, and dragged them into a house (not the *skasnai*) and behind a curtain. In the evening all the people, regardless of membership in the society, assembled in the *skasnai* to exorcise the spirit that possessed the initiates.
>
> The female members danced in their various characters, and then the initiates, led in through the front door by their attendants, danced round the fire and retired behind the curtain. They reappeared and performed several times in different costumes until they were "tamed." The night was passed in dancing and performing sleight-of-hand tricks such as seemingly decapitating an initiate and restoring his life.

Each dancing society had its own distinctive features (PLATES 48, 49). Some societies were the exclusive right of particular village chiefs and not widely distributed on Haida Gwaii. Swanton and Curtis interviewed many informants sufficiently long after the passing of the societies that they revealed some facts which otherwise would have been kept secret.

Swanton (1905:16) claims that the secret societies were merged with the shamanic beliefs of the Haida:

> Just as a shaman was supposed to be inspired by some supernatural being who "spoke," or, as they generally preferred to translate it to me, "came through" him, so the U'lala spirit, the Dog-eating spirit, the Grisly-Bear spirit, and so on, "came through" the secret-society novice.

One of the main societies was the Ulala (or Wilala), similar to the Hamatsa (or Cannibal) among the Kwakwaka'wakw (or Kwakiutl), which was danced only by men. A long pole with a crossbar projected through the roof from behind the dance curtain and had cedar bark streamers suspended from it. This pole was rotated to signal to those outside that the Ulala was about to emerge. According to Curtis (1916:145), "Various masks were worn by Ulala, depending on the supposed source of his supernatural power."

Much of what shocked and repelled the early missionaries about the winter dances was the stagecraft, which they took very literally. Curtis (1916:144) describes some such enactments by the Ulala:

> He made the gestures and facial expressions of the Hamatsa, and pretended to bite either forearm of several persons. Actually he did not bite at all. Those who were to be "bitten" had previously raised a blister on the forearm by burning cedar-bark over a round spot, so that after the "biting" they could exhibit a raw wound. Many of the oldest men have numerous such scars extending along the arm.
>
> On appearing at the edge of the woods, Ulala mounted a mortuary hut and took out an image closely resembling a corpse. It was covered with the dark skins of scoters, and looked much like a dried, mouldy corpse. Inside the belly was a mass of cooked spruce-bast, or a long string of flour paste colored bluish so as to resemble intestines. Sometimes the initiate would tear the belly skin open and there on the beach devour the contents, but usually the "corpse" was taken from him and carried into the house, where he ate and passed portions among the other Ulala.

MASKS

Secret societies and their performances began to disappear with the arrival of the missionaries in the mid-1870s. A photograph documents the participants in the last secret society dances at Skidegate in the 1880s (PLATE 124), showing some of the young women wearing masks while others wear frontlets or have painted their faces (PLATES 50, 51).

Among the Haida, masks were used mostly by members of the secret societies (PLATES 1, 52 to 56, 58 to 71). Secret society dances frequently used both masks and puppets to represent wild spirits of the woods, which the Haida called *gagiid*. They are distinguished by an emaciated or wrinkled face and grimacing mouth, and are often blue-green in colour, to indicate that they portray a person who has narrowly escaped drowning and whose flesh has gone cold from long exposure in cold water (PLATES 56, 57).

Like their Tsimshian neighbours, the Haida also employed masks in potlatch performances to illustrate the spirit beings (*geni loci*) encountered by their ancestors. Unfortunately, much less is known about such supernatural being masks among the Haida than about the *nox nox* (or supernatural spirit) masks of the Tsimshian, who to this day have maintained their traditions in some interior villages.

PLATE 50

This deerskin bag, which held powdered red ochre for paint used in a variety of ceremonies, has seen much wear. The double-headed Thunderbird on the front is a rarity among the Haida, who usually portray it with a single head. It is very similar in form to a tattoo design and may have been used as such by the owner. *Collected from Skidegate between 1890 and 1904 by Charles F. Newcombe.* CMC VII-B-538 (S92-4235)

PLATE 51

The style of the painting on this deerskin bag (used to store red ochre for paint) is truly outstanding and was done by an unknown master artist of the middle of the last century. On the bag are two classic opposites: the Thunderbird, which is the supreme sky being, and the Killer Whale, which is one manifestation of the Chief of the Seas. *Collected at Skidegate between 1890 and 1904 by Charles F. Newcombe.* CMC VII-B-537 (S92-4233)

The influence of the tourist market on Haida mask-making is difficult to evaluate. After the 1840s, masks and argillite carvings were the items most sought after by seamen, traders and tourists, and probably several thousand Haida masks are held in private and museum collections around the world. Deciding which masks were made for traditional use rather than for sale is largely a matter of judgement. Indicators of actual use include signs of wear on the leather ties and interior surface, the functionality of the eyeholes, the allowance for facial fit for wearing, evidence of attachment of headcloths or animal fur that was stripped off before sale, and traces of glue and down or cedar bark. The opposite factors such as no means for attaching the mask to the wearer's head, no preparation of the interior to avoid rubbing the wearer's nose and no functional eyeholes indicate that a mask was made for tourists.

Famous artists like Simeon Stiltla and Charles Edenshaw are known to have made masks for ceremonial use. One such example is the elaborate transformation mask by Charles Edenshaw now in the Pitt Rivers Museum at Oxford University.

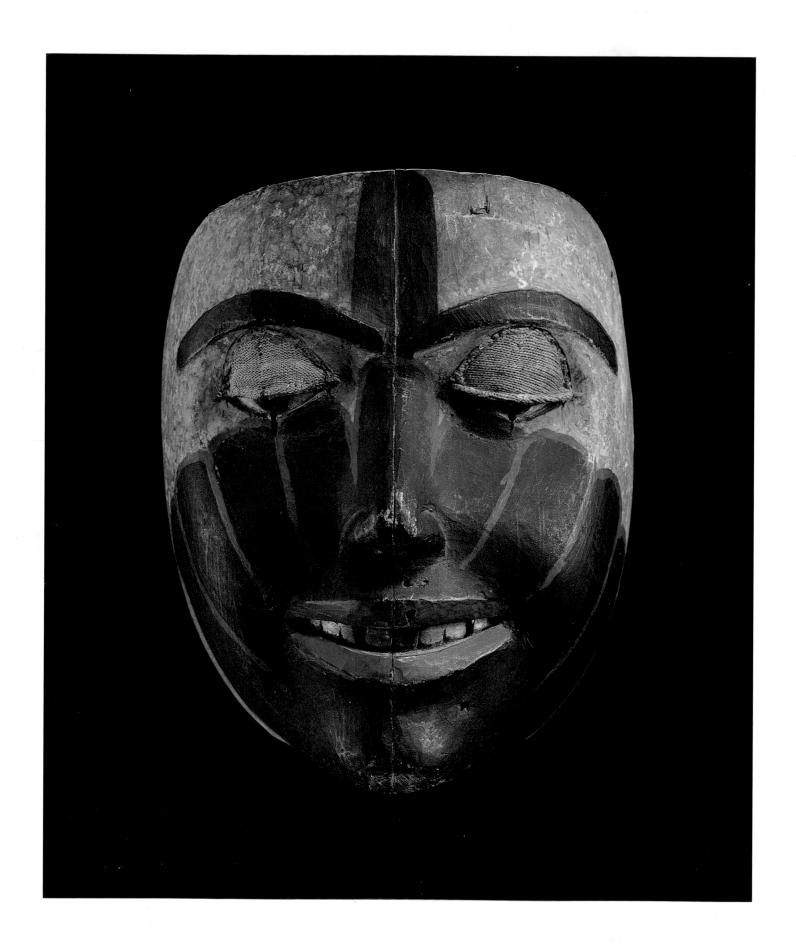

PLATE 54

A secret society mask made by Simeon Stiltla (1833–1883). Raven feather patterns are painted around the mouth. The face is fuller than on most of this artist's works, but the narrow eyebrows, pointed chin and movable eyes are all characteristic of his style. *Collected at Masset before 1884 by Alexander McKenzie of the Hudson's Bay Company.* CMC VII-B-1 (S92-4160)

PLATE 55

A portrait mask by Simeon Stiltla of an old woman wearing a large labret. Streamers of red wool originally decorated the ears. Stiltla usually incised the hair in plaited grooves to look like the folk carvings made by sailors on New England ships, but on this rare example he painted the hair pattern, perhaps to differentiate it from the wrinkles on the old woman's face. *Collected at Masset before 1884 by Alexander McKenzie of the Hudson's Bay Company.* CMC VII-B-7 (S92-4163)

PLATE 56

This mask used in secret
society dances represents a
gagiid, or wild spirit of the
woods, someone who narrowly
escaped drowning but whose
flesh has changed colour from
long exposure in cold water.
*Collected on Haida Gwaii in
1879 by Israel W. Powell.* CMC
VII-B-109 (s92-4186)

PLATE 57

The head of a *gagiid* doll used
in secret society dances. The
cloth body as well as the
wooden hands and feet have
been lost. *Collected at Masset
before 1900 by Charles F.
Newcombe.* CMC VII-B-526
(s94-6728)

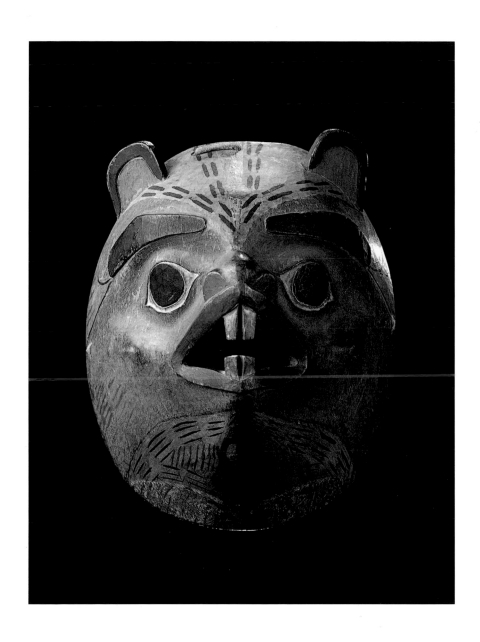

PLATE 58

This very fine mask made in the middle of the nineteenth century once had a moustache and goatee made of bear fur. *Collected on Haida Gwaii (probably Skidegate) in 1879 by Israel W. Powell.* CMC VII-B-3 (s85-3270)

PLATE 59

The relatively small upper incisors of this Marmot mask and the lack of a stick in its mouth distinguish it from a Beaver. *Collected by Alexander McKenzie of the Hudson's Bay Company, who commented it was used in a social dance at a house-warming potlatch in Masset before 1884.* CMC VII-B-136a (s85-3277)

PLATE 60

This forehead mask represents
a Beaver characteristically
gnawing a stick, which it holds
with humanlike hands. There
is abalone shell inlay on the
teeth and eyes, and streamers
of human hair. Some
Tsimshian influence is evident
in the form and decoration of
the eyebrows. *Collected on
Haida Gwaii in 1879 by Israel
W. Powell.* CMC VII-B-17 (S92-
4168)

PLATE 61

This dance mask dating from
about 1860 has unusual red
eyes, with peepholes beside
each pupil rather than in the
centre of them, lending a
blank or neutral expression to
the face. Red cedar bark and
eagle down are still attached.
*Collected on Haida Gwaii in
1879 by Israel W. Powell.* CMC
VII-B-4 (S92-4161)

PLATE 62 (facing page)
A dance mask with a movable
attachment of a White
Squirrel on top. The style is
markedly Tsimshian,
including the dashed and
crosshatched zones on the face,
as well as the White Squirrel
crest. Masks like this one were
probably acquired by the
Haida in trade at Fort
Simpson. *Collected on Haida
Gwaii in 1879 by Israel W.
Powell.* CMC VII-B-21 (S92-4171)

PLATE 63
A mask with unusually large
eyeholes, peaked eyebrows and
thick lips. It appears to have
been made by the same artist
as the masks in PLATES 64, 65,
66, 67. The extensive face
painting on it is crudely done
and gives no indication of
what it represents. *Collected on
Haida Gwaii (probably at
Skidegate) in 1879 by Israel W.
Powell.* CMC VII-B-135 (S92-
4195)

PLATE 64
A Moon mask with painted
eyebrows and delicate
feminine features. *Collected on
Haida Gwaii (probably at
Skidegate) in 1879 by Israel W.
Powell.* CMC VII-B-9 (S85-3273)

PLATE 65

On the top of this mask of a supernatural Killer Whale is a dorsal fin, which can be pulled upright with hidden strings. The lower jaw is also movable. Other stylistic features such as the peaked eyebrows, large eye openings and thick lips indicate it is also by the same artist who made the masks in PLATES 63, 64, 66, 67. CMC VII-B-13 (S94-6724)

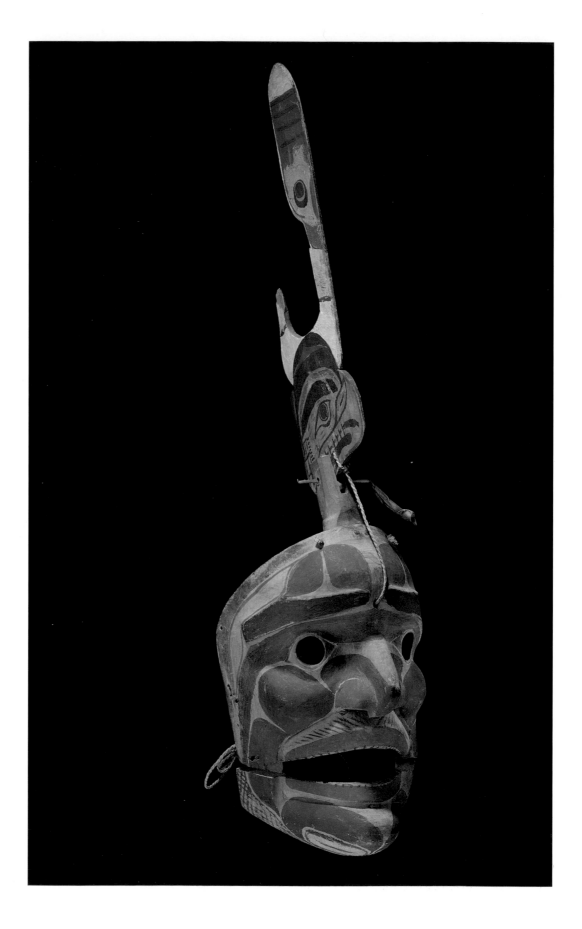

PLATE 66

A Moon mask with robust male features. There are traces of a cloth hood that was once attached to it. The style of a broad face and thick lips looks is similar to Heiltsuk masks but may have been used by Haida to suggest the full face of the Moon. *Collected on Haida Gwaii (probably Skidegate) in 1879 by Israel W. Powell.* CMC VII-B-19 (S92-4170)

PLATE 67A, 67B

This spectacular transformation mask, when closed, represents an Eagle or Thunderbird; open (*right*), it portrays the Moon. Human hair attachments add to the drama of the powerfully serene face of a supernatural being. The transformation of the mask is accomplished by pulling cords attached to the hinged panels that extend to form the corona. *Collected on Haida Gwaii (probably at Skidegate) in 1879 by Israel W. Powell.* CMC VII-B-20 (s86-386 closed, s86-387 open)

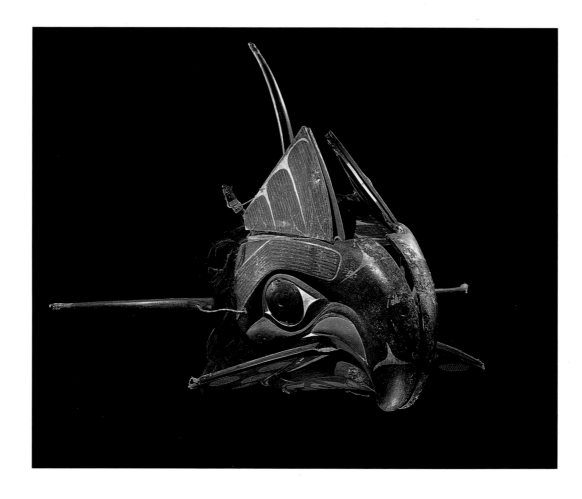

An unusual dance mask of a supernatural being whose identity is now lost. The lips are edged with copper, and the beard is bear fur. A wig of human hair completes the eclectic effect. *Collected on Haida Gwaii in 1879 by Israel W. Powell.* CMC VII-B-10 (S92-4164)

This very powerful mask was clearly used in ceremonies and still has remnants of down nailed to the chin. The meaning of the three harpoons emerging from the face is unknown, but they were probably inserted into holes in the mask at a special point in the performance. *Collected at Masset before 1884 by Alexander McKenzie of the Hudson's Bay Company.* CMC VII-B-2 (S85-3269)

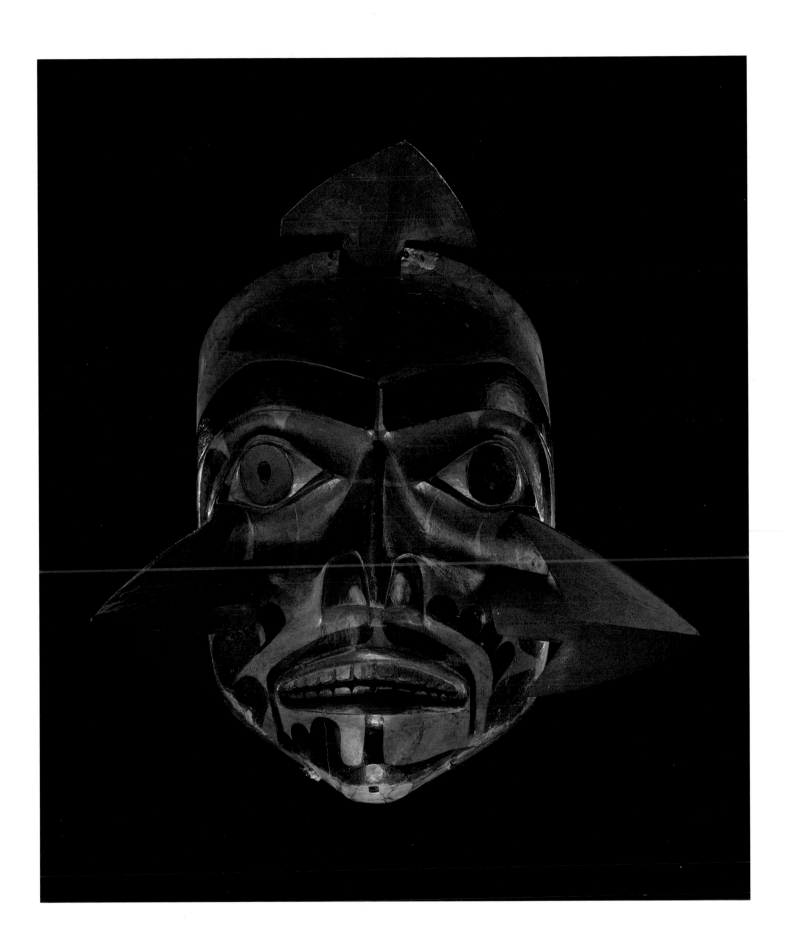

PLATE 70

A secret society dance mask portraying a Mosquito. Nail holes at the top indicate it once had fur or feather attachments and was used in ceremonies. *Purchased from the A. Aaronson collection in 1899 but probably acquired earlier at Masset by James Deans.* CMC VII-B-704 (S92-4257)

PLATE 71

On this secret society dance mask of a hawklike bird, the eyes are trimmed with metal plates, and there are leather-hinged side panels that could be manipulated by the dancer. Signs of wear inside the mask indicate it was used in many performances. *Collected on Haida Gwaii in 1879 by Israel W. Powell.* CMC VII-B-24 (S92-4176)

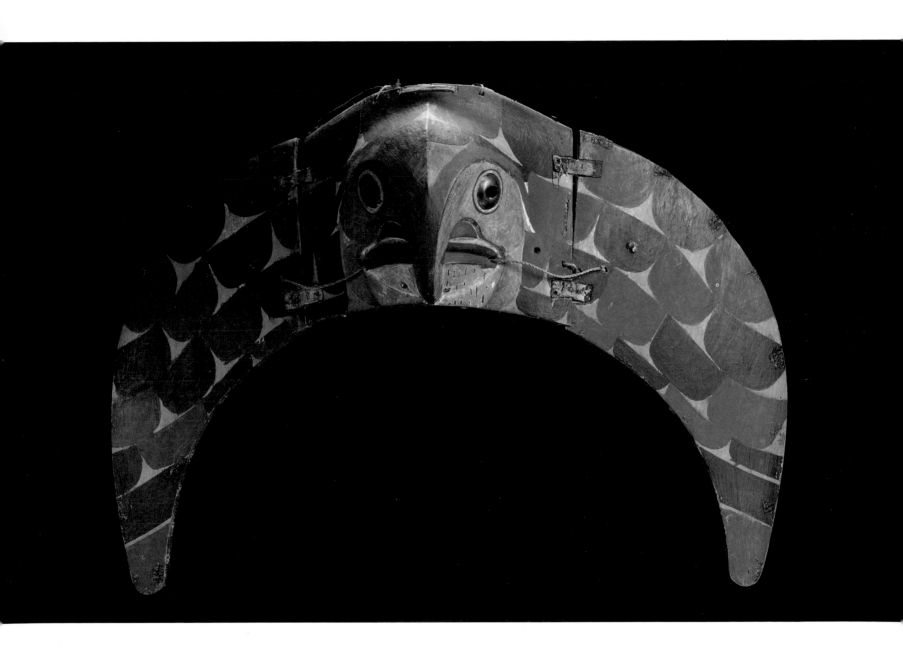

LUCK OF THE GAMBLER

The Haida had several popular games that involved gambling, and a lull in any social activity was a good reason to play. One was a simple game similar to pickup sticks. The thin playing sticks were quickly made and never decorated, so they were not sought by collectors and no examples are preserved in museums.

Another game consisted of three sets of sticks, named after different animals or birds, which, according to Charles F. Newcombe (1902:MS), were known only to the owner and his family. The sticks have rings and spiral markings to distinguish them, but the most elaborate sets are a veritable gallery of Haida art and may contain fifty or more unique drawings (PLATE 72). The sticks were made of hard maple and were decorated by carving, painting and pyro-engraving with a hot poker; many were inlaid with abalone shell or copper. The burning-in of designs with a hot poker demanded different skills from Haida artists, who responded admirably to the challenge. The drawings are difficult to appreciate at first glance, since they are wrapped completely around the sticks, which must be rotated slowly to unlock their form. Some have jumping shaman figures that resemble an animated cartoon; as the stick is rotated, one shaman after another jumps into view. Flying birds are also common, along with jumping killer whales.

There are also scores of examples of very complex scenes such as war parties in canoes, sea otter hunters in action, or fishermen and their catch—each entire composition no more than 2 cm (¾ inch) in length. These gaming pieces seem to offer the only decorative field in which the Haida artist felt free to become truly documentary. Drawings of half a dozen sets of these decorated sticks have been published by Franz Boas (1927:figs. 200, 201), Swanton (1905:149–54) and others, but many await study. George T. Emmons (no date) recorded in meticulous detail the identifications by a Tlingit owner of a full set of sticks now in the National Museum of the American Indian.

These gambling sticks were used on a special leather mat that was often decorated with painted or pyro-engraved images that appear to be regular crests. This is appropriate, since crests are generally considered to bring good fortune to those who have the inherited the right to use them.

PLATE 72

A set of Haida gambling sticks decorated with pyro-engraved crest images. They were kept in the painted deerskin bag. *Collected at the Nass River village of Gitlaxdimiks in 1905 by Charles F. Newcombe.* CMC VII-C-142 (S92-4313)

Like other north coast peoples, the Haida believed that the souls of the deceased travelled first to the sky world in their cycle of reincarnation (Swanton 1905:35). Both prayers and souls could be helped on their journey by means of smoke rising from the central hearth of the house or by smoke rising from pipes. Prior to contact, the Haida used local tobacco. Pipe smoking became strongly associated with the extraordinary powers initially attributed to Europeans, particularly firearms, which not only smoked but brought instant injury or death. Many early pipes were made from the walnut of gunstocks and parts of gun barrels in order to capture and transfer the power of guns to pipes (PLATE 73).

At some point, argillite replaced recycled gun parts for the making of pipes, but fixing upon a date for the beginning of argillite carving has been something of a challenge to scholars. One clue was found by archaeologist Knut Fladmark (1973:90) of Simon Fraser University, who discovered a chiefly burial inside a house floor at Lawn Hill, on the east coast south of Rose Spit. A well-sculpted argillite pipe of a clam with a human face on it is related to this burial, which associated trade goods date to before 1820.

Next to totem poles, argillite carvings are probably the best known art form of the Haida (Barbeau 1944, 1954, 1957; Macnair and Hoover 1984; Sheehan 1981; Wright 1985). They alone produced works in argillite, since they controlled the supply of the soft black stone, which came from Slatechuck Creek on a mountainside near the village of Skidegate. Argillaceous slate does occur elsewhere on the Northwest Coast, but the lustrous black variety found near Skidegate is unique. Although Skidegate controlled the supply of argillite, it was Masset artists who produced some of the most famous pieces. A much inferior form of the stone, red in colour with mottled yellowish inclusions, occurs as surface boulders around Masset. Works made of this stone can be considered as invariably coming from there, for it was used only by Masset artists who sometimes did not find it convenient to travel to Skidegate to obtain prime black argillite.

The ability of Haida artists to work in stone is well documented in prehistoric carvings, particularly tobacco mortars and pestles (PLATES 74, 75). One interesting stone bowl, probably dating from the eighteenth century, depicts a Dragonfly carrying a human, possibly in reference to myths about Dragonflies transporting human souls. A later piece in argillite on the same theme portrays a human figure riding on the back of a Dragonfly.

The transition of argillite pipes from a ceremonial function to an item of exchange or sale is quite clear. By the 1830s, the sea otter trade that had brought the Haida so much wealth so quickly was over. However, as ships engaged in the trade for other furs continued to ply the coast, the Haida attempted to find substitutes for sea otter pelts by offering potatoes as well as fresh and dried fish. The sale of artworks also became increasingly important to the Haida economy. When the Hudson's Bay Company established a trading post at Fort Simpson on the mainland, British gunboats replaced maritime traders as customers to a large extent. Hundreds of pieces of carved argillite were purchased and taken home as

PLATE 73

On this wooden pipe with a brass bowl, the design of the Raven (with another bird's head on its tail) is very similar to one on a Raven rattle (PLATE 19), with the notable absence of the human figure on its back. *Purchased from Douglas Ewing of New York City in 1976.* CMC VII-B-1659 (S92-4313)

94

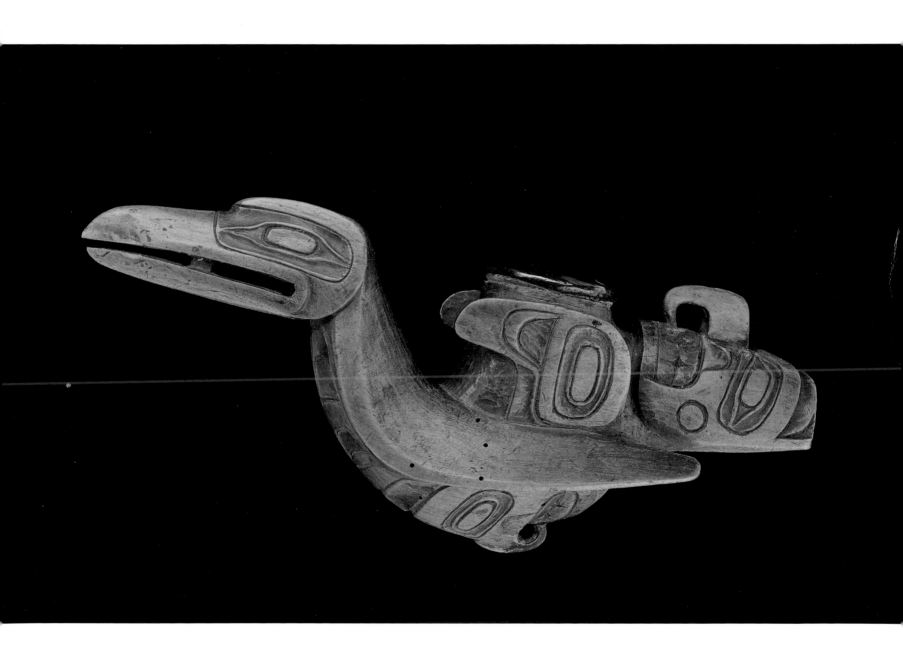

souvenirs by sailors from New England, Britain and elsewhere.

When Reverend Jonathan Green (1915:86) stayed near Skidegate in 1829, he noted that "pipes which the Haida make of a kind of slate stone are curiously wrought." Art historian Robin Wright (1985) has documented in detail the florescence of the panel pipe form, which lost its original funeral function and became a medium for the expression of myths and even for the recording of historical events.

Although panel pipes were the first form of argillite carving sold to tourists, the Haida soon began making and ornamenting other objects that appealed to Europeans. Dishes were particularly successful, since Victorians delighted in displaying plates, bowls and platters in cabinets, on sideboards and on special rails around their parlours (PLATES 76, 154, 157, 158). Pipes appealed enormously to seamen, while plates and platters were equally attractive to their sweethearts back home.

Throughout the 1850s, the design of panel pipes became more baroque. Other forms of pipes, more in the European style but with Haida images, were also produced, along with ever more elaborate plates and platters. It is worth noting that in Britain during the Victorian era, jet carving was popular. Jet is a type of metamorphosed coal that occurs in association with many coal deposits in Britain, and crippled or retired miners often took up jet carving after they could no longer work. The jet jewellery and figurines they produced as a livelihood were well suited to the funeral rituals and long mourning periods of the time. This may explain why the lustrous black carvings of the Haida, especially of familiar forms like pipes, mugs, dishes and platters, were readily accepted by the people of Victorian Britain. Haida argillite carvings, along with African carvings in ebony, found ready markets throughout the Victorian age.

Miniature totem poles in argillite were introduced in the 1860s and became increasingly popular in the 1870s and 1880s. Reverend William H. Collison, a missionary, provides a rare note about the argillite carving that had by the 1870s become a major source of income to the people of Skidegate (in Lillard 1981:173):

> The Haida of Skidegate possess a deposit of black stone [argillite] in the vicinity of their village, from which they obtain material to keep them engaged, during their spare moments, in designing and carving a variety of articles for sale. Miniature totem poles for mantelpiece ornaments, of various sizes, large and small dishes, sometimes inlaid with abalone and ornamented with rows of the teeth of marine animals and fishes and many other designs, are carved, and then smoothed by rubbing them with the dried skin of the shark. During the winter this tribe continues to prepare a stock of ornamental articles from this black stone, which takes a fine polish, and brings them a good sum of money when sold at various centres. The possession of this stone is quite a treasure to them, as it tends to preserve and improve the art of carving and designing amongst them, besides bringing in a revenue.

By the turn of the century, the wide dispersal of tens of thousands of argillite carvings

PLATE 74
A sandstone mortar for grinding burned clamshells to make lime, which was then mixed with flakes of dried native tobacco leaves; the lime chemically released the psychogenic compounds in the tobacco, much like the use of lime and betel nut in southeast Asia and other parts of the Pacific. The hands holding the stick that identify this as a Beaver emerge from the creature's own mouth, presumably to keep the sculpture very compact since more anatomically correct arms would easily break off.
Collected on Haida Gwaii in 1879 by Israel W. Powell. CMC XII-B-318 (S91-946)

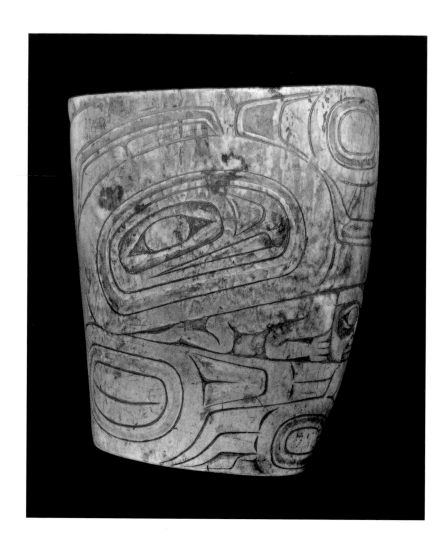

PLATE 75

A mortar of walrus ivory
engraved with an image of the
Raven holding a human being
in its beak. Pieces of burned
clamshell were crushed in this
mortar to make lime for use
with tobacco. *Collected at
Masset before 1884 by James
Deans for Dr. W. F. Tolmie of
the Hudson's Bay Company.*
CMC VII-B-1001 (S92-4292)

PLATE 76

An argillite dish made circa
1835 depicts European women
apparently dancing, and it is
also adorned with the leaves
and berries of the native Haida
tobacco plant. Rosettes and
chrysanthemumlike motifs are
also common in the work of
this unnamed artist. Another
plate by the same carver is in
the Bristol Museum in
England (Drew and Wilson
1980:205, top). CMC VII-C-1036
(S92-4293)

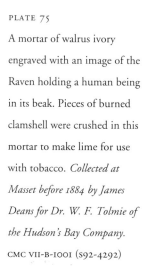

had led to the recognition by discerning collectors of the works of particular artists like
Charles Edenshaw and John Cross. John Cross was trained first in tattooing in the 1870s
(Barbeau 1957:124–25) and later turned his talents to argillite carving. No argillite carvings
were signed, although a few have artists' names written on them by collectors themselves.

Thomas Deasey, the federal government Indian agent at Masset, assembled hundreds of
examples of the works of many Masset artists early this century. His collection was donated
to the Florida State Museum in Gainesville (PLATE 153).

Argillite carving went into decline after the First World War until the 1950s and was rele-
gated to a minor place in the tourist market. The style of the poles was limited to the repeti-
tion of a narrow range of crests and figures compared to the innovative period in the last
century. Now, most of the poles for sale in shops in Vancouver and Victoria are cast in simu-
lated argillite and are not even made by Haida artisans.

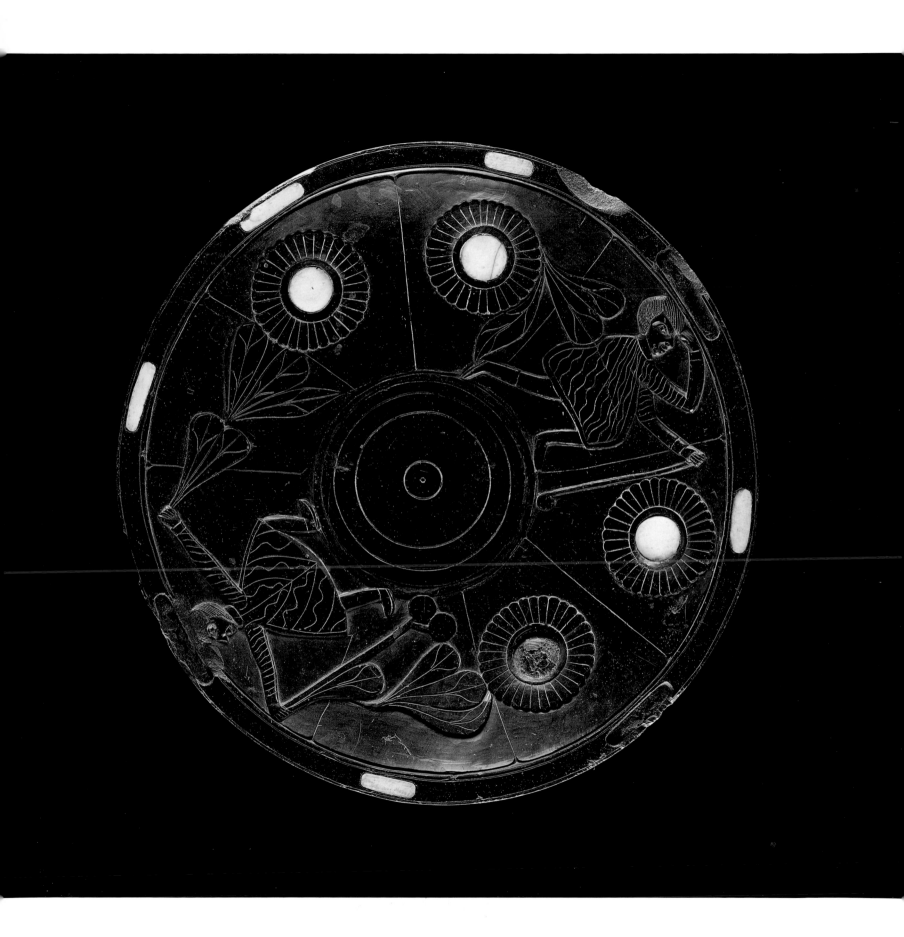

HOUSES

Permanent Haida villages consisted of one or more rows of houses strung along a beach. Double-row villages were quite common, but villages with up to five rows of houses existed only in myth time. Generally the house owned by the town chief was larger than the rest and stood near the middle of the village.

The most extensive early reconnaissance of north coast native villages was carried out by Ensign Albert Niblack, who first visited them during tours of duty with the U.S. Navy. Later, in the 1880s, he returned for a number of years to photograph and record them in detail for the Smithsonian Institution. He was most impressed by the houses built by the Haida (Niblack 1890:384):

> Their houses are exceptionally well constructed, and the custom of erecting the carved column in contact with the front of the house and cutting a circular doorway through both, seems to be nowhere so universally practiced.

According to ancient myth, the house was one of the main contributions that the Raven made to Haida life after he stole the idea from the Beaver (Robert Davidson in Thom 1994:19). The house was the centre of Haida social, political and economic life. Certain aspects and themes related to the house call for some elaboration in order to better understand the setting within which all Haida art was created and used. The subject of houses and their decoration is dealt with extensively in the book *Haida Monumental Art* (MacDonald 1983).

Haida houses were constructed of western red cedar with a framework of stout corner posts that supported massive beams. The frame was clad with wide planks. The tools required for building houses included sledgehammers, adzes, hand mauls and wedges for splitting wood. Most housebuilding tools were not decorated, but a few examples in the collection of the Canadian Museum of Civilization are quite remarkable (PLATES 77,78).

Small houses averaged 6 by 9 m (20 by 30 feet) and were occupied by thirty to forty closely related family members, while large houses were up to 15 by 18 m (50 by 60 feet) with twice as many residents, including immediate family and slaves. The ideal house had a large pit in the central area, often lined with a vertical box structure of massive planks. The hearth occupied the centre, directly under a smokehole, which had a plank flap that could be moved

PLATE 77

An elaborately carved basalt hand maul that was used for driving wooden wedges into red cedar logs to split off planks. James Deans identifies the lower face as that of a Bear, with the naturalistic head of a hunter above. The hunter's conical hat forms the traditional top of a nipple-top maul, suggesting this may have been an old maul that was later enhanced with a carved design. The accession record claims it was once in the collection of Sir Matthew Begbie, chief justice of British Columbia. *Acquired with the A. Aaronson collection in 1899, but probably originally collected by James Deans in the early 1890s on Haida Gwaii.* CMC VII-B-908 (s82-269) with ropes to control the draft for the fire. Usually the house of the town chief had the largest or deepest housepit. The roofs of houses belonging to people of rank were covered with overlapping planks, anchored in placed with large rocks. The houses of poorer people and canoe sheds had roofs of cedar bark that had to be replaced frequently.

The people of the northern and southern regions of Haida Gwaii have different approaches to house construction. In the north, including the villages of the Prince of Wales archipelago, Haida houses resemble the large gable-roofed plank structures found throughout other north coast villages. This house has an *internal* frame consisting of four or more massive vertical posts spanned by equally massive round beams up to 15 m (50 feet) or more in length, covered with a cladding of wide planks.

In the south, houses have an *external* frame, with plank cladding that fits precisely between the parallel timbers of the house frame. This more elaborate style of house, with mortice and tenon joints and low-tolerance carpentry, probably did not develop until steel tools became available in the late eighteenth century. The greatest incidence of the exterior frame house occurs at the village of Ninstints at the southern tip of Haida Gwaii.

A third type of house occurs predominantly among the Kaigani Haida of the Prince of Wales archi-

pelago in Alaska. It is a blend of the two basic styles, in having both an interior frame based on four massive posts as well as a system for the walls and gables supported by four smaller exterior corner posts. Large houses, like that of Chief Skowl at Kasaan village, have a heavy horizontal timber between the front corner posts (repeated at the back wall) that effectively divides the cladding on the front and back gables above and below this beam into shorter boards.

The terms applied to a house's structural members are the same as for the bones of a human skeleton, or more specifically the bones of the collective ancestor. The two front vertical support posts are the arm bones, the two rear posts are the leg bones, the longitudinal beams are the backbone, the rafters are the ribs, and the exterior cladding is the skin. The inhabitants are the spirit force of the ancestor/house.

In addition to being a place of shelter, the house had a cosmological meaning for the

Haida, who thought of the house as a very large box and often decorated its walls to coincide with the images used on boxes. The concept of boxes within boxes is central to Haida beliefs about containers and the spiritual beings who safeguard their precious contents.

The wealth contained by the house-sized box was in the form of human souls. The Haida believed that the fish stored in food boxes retained their souls until they were consumed, when their souls were released to become new fish and continue the cycle. Similarly, a house protected the souls of its inhabitants until they died, whereby their souls were released to newborn members of the family. The Haida were always concerned to know which child had inherited the soul of a recently deceased relative and would search the faces and actions of the newborn to determine that affiliation. The deceased were placed in burial boxes in mortuary houses or on posts, as close as tolerable to the house of their surviving kin (PLATES 79, 80). Reverend William H. Collison (in Lillard 1981:86) comments on this after his first night in a house at Masset village:

> When opening my door the following morning, I was startled at receiving a smart lash as though from a whip on the side of my face. Looking up to see the cause, I perceived that the wind had blown the side out of a mortuary chest, which was supported by two great posts. In this receptacle lay the skeleton of a woman, her long black hair was being blown to and fro by the wind as it hung down fully three feet from the scalp.

The Haida viewed the universe as a large house (the World Box or World House), with the sides being the four cardinal directions. After the Raven brought the sun to this World Box from another box in the house of the Sky Chief, the sun entered the World House each day and passed over its roof at night. The stars were sunlight shining through holes in roof of the World House. The seasons were tracked by marking the position of the sun at daybreak on the wall opposite the hole where the sunlight entered.

Through the middle of each house ran an axis that centred the resident family at the centre of the world, where the contact between the various levels of the universe was the greatest. The smoke from the household fire signified this axis of conjunction of various worlds and the hearth was the site of daily prayers to the supernatural forces that determined people's destiny. The houses of important chiefs had a succession of box-shaped pits extending symbolically down into the underworld. The living compartment of the chief was like a smaller box at the back of the house.

Not a single complete original Haida dwelling survives, but there are historical photographs of about four hundred Haida houses in twenty-five villages, taken in the last half of the nineteenth century. In addition, nearly one hundred house models survive in museum collections. The Field Museum in Chicago has the entire village of Skidegate, some thirty houses in model form, commissioned by James Deans for the Columbian World Exposition in Chicago in 1893 (PLATE 81).

Deans spent considerable time in Skidegate in the 1880s and was able to recruit craftsmen from each lineage group to make models of the houses connected to their families. It must have been a terrific undertaking on his part to negotiate the rights, fees, and schedules of so many artists to deliver the complete model within a year. The model even has carvings of figures engaged in various rituals from funeral ceremonies to potlatches, and the house belonging to Chief Skidegate includes a detailed reconstruction of the interior house pit.

Another excellent piece that is part of the model of Skidegate village is the mortuary that stood behind Chief Skidegate's house. It is a shedlike building with a painted housefront depicting a Wasgo (or Sea Wolf) that once lived in a lake behind Skidegate. When its roof is removed, stacks of burial chests are revealed, including the highly decorated ones of former Chiefs Skidegate resting on a huge carving of a Wasgo. Such supports (called *manda'a* by the Haida) were often placed at the foot of the mortuary post to which the chief's burial box was moved two years after his death (PLATE 166). Many of these carved supports can be seen in historical photos of Haida villages.

Housefront Paintings

Despite the fact that all of the mainland tribes between Vancouver Island and central Alaska had painted housefronts, they were rare among the Haida. This is surprising, since the Haida were the most accomplished artists on the coast in flat design as applied to canoes, chiefs' seats and storage chests. One example from the Skidegate area of Haida Gwaii is on the

PLATE 80

This central panel from a double-post mortuary in Skidegate village portrays the Grizzly Bear with a protruding tongue and prominent ears. *Collected circa 1900 by Charles F. Newcombe.* CMC VII-B-668 (S92-4246)

105

house of Chief Gold, who together with his wife was the first to report the discovery of gold on the islands to Albert Edward Edenshaw in 1849. At the time, Chief Gold was head chief of Kaisun village, but later he moved his people to Haina village (now New Gold Harbour) near Skidegate. He rebuilt his own house at First Beach between Skidegate and Haina to maintain ancient rights of his family to that site.

When Chief Gold rebuilt his house, he added a housefront that follows the precise template of many such paintings among the Tsimshian, especially popular at Fort Simpson (PLATE 82). That pattern consists of a Master of Souls flat design with multiple faces in the eyes and human figures in the mouth. The remarkable feature of the housefront is the profile of Thunderbird flanking each side of the main design. Since the Haida from the Skidegate area travelled regularly to Fort Simpson to trade, Chief Gold may have either received the right to use the pattern as a gift or purchased it from a Tsimshian chief. Chief Gold subsequently commissioned a local Haida artist to execute this housefront painting. Bill Holm (1981:199) convincingly argues that this artist is also "the Master of the Chicago Settee." The closest Tsimshian example is the house of Chief Skagwait, the second-highest in rank to Chief Legaic at Fort Simpson. In Haida society, Chief Gold had a comparable position as second in rank to Chief Skidegate. Chief Gold added a distinctive Haida touch by putting his Moon-Hawk crest on the gable of his house.

Another Haida housefront painting exists only as a photograph of a collection of boards from an exquisite housefront, assembled somewhat randomly on a chief's grave in the cemetery of the Kaigani Haida village of Howkan in Alaska. In the photo, about a quarter of the painted boards are missing, most are out of order, and some are upside-down (PLATE 148). A number of detailed features of this painting suggest that it was commissioned from an artist at Fort Simpson, as it closely resembles about ten other housefronts from that town. Collectively, these are the finest corpus of two-dimensional design from the Northwest Coast.

There is evidence of two other painted housefronts in Skidegate village proper. The first belonged to the town chief, Skidegate, whom collector James G. Swan (1893:MS 49) referred to as "Skidegate the Great," the highest-ranking chief on the central and southern islands and equal in rank to Chief Wiah of Masset. We know of this housefront painting only from a model, which probably exaggerates reality. The model depicts a Konankada flat design, almost identical to that on many carved storage chests. There are no flanking bird or animal figures as in the Tsimshian examples, but Killer Whale designs are painted on the side walls of the model. In concept, this design is comparable to the Tsimshian housefront painting from Fort Simpson now in the Smithsonian Museum. This assemblage has been interpreted as the Tsimshian figure Hakulack, a variant of Gonankadet (or Konankada), flanked by two Killer Whales (MacDonald 1981:230, fig. 5).

Although nothing has survived of the housefront painting owned by Chief Skidegate, historical photos of his house reveal that it had no frontal pole (although that of his predecessor stood nearby). The housefront was an unusually plain one for such a high-ranking chief, and the implication is that it was decorated for potlatches by the erection of a painted plank

PLATE 81

This model of Skidegate village was commissioned for the Columbian World Exposition in Chicago in 1893. James Deans hired most of the artists active in Skidegate at the time to make models of their own lineage houses.

PLATE 82

A rare example of a painted housefront from Moon House, which Chief Gold built at First Beach near Skidegate. According to Bill Holm (1981:197), the painting was done by the unknown artist referred to as "the Master of the Chicago Settee." The Moon-Hawk plaque at the top, which was moved by Chief Gold from his previous house at Kaisun village, is now in the Field Museum. *Photograph by Richard Maynard, 1881.*

PLATE 83

This is a model of Chief Giatlins's Grizzly Bear's Mouth House, one of the most unusual buildings in Skidegate. The housefront was sculpted as well as painted, particularly the snout of the Bear, which protruded out quite a way from the painted portion. Two oval doorways were positioned at the corners of the Bear's mouth. The Eagles on the corner posts are crests that belong to the owner's wife. The model was made about 1890 by John Robson, a leading Skidegate carver who inherited the house. *Acquired at Skidegate before 1900 for the Lord Bossom collection.* CMC VII-B-1556 (S92-4309)

PLATE 84

House models were a favourite
souvenir of early tourists, and
Haida carvers embellished
them with every conceivable
decoration. This one made by
a Kaigani Haida artist in the
1890s has carved frontal and
corner poles, carved rafter ends
and even a housefront painting
of the Raven in opposing
profiles. No such house was
ever built. *Acquired in
southeast Alaska before 1900 by
George T. Emmons for the Lord
Bossom collection.* CMC VII-X-
1280 (s94-6741)

housefront screen—and possibly additional painted screens on the sides of the house—as shown on the Field Museum model of the village (PLATE 81).

The second Skidegate decorated housefront is considerably different. Grizzly Bear's Mouth House, owned by Chief Giatlins, was a six-beam structure in which the decoration was both carved and painted onto the thick vertical planks that were inserted into the gables of the housefront (MacDonald 1983:45, house 5). Although this housefront technically was removable, it was so integrated into the structure that it was probably left in place permanently.

Skidegate artist John Robson (a later Chief Giatlins) made two models of Grizzly Bear's Mouth House that survive, one in the Canadian Museum of Civilization (PLATE 83) and the other in the Field Museum. The former coincides closely with the photo of the house taken in 1878 by George M. Dawson, who was sent by the federal government to survey the central and northern coast of British Columbia in the late 1870s. A memorial pole in front of this house was commissioned by John Robson in memory of his wife Qwa'Kuna, the mother of Charles Edenshaw.

There are no known housefront paintings among the Kaigani Haida of Alaska, with the exception of the funeral monument at Howkan (PLATE 148). However, there are some Kaigani house models with painted front panels as well as totem poles. No historical photo confirms this combination, so the models may have been made more for tourist appeal than as an authentic record. One house model acquired by the collector Lord Bossom has on it every possible decoration (PLATE 84).

Carved Interior Poles and Posts

The oldest form of interior carved crest poles in Haida houses was probably the pair of matched posts that stood at the back wall under the central beams. Frequently, there was but a single crest figure on each of these posts (PLATE 85), such as a Bear, Whale, Raven, Sea Lion or human, though in some houses, like that of Chief Skowl at Kasaan, all four support posts are elaborately carved. These carved house posts are typical of both Tlingit and Tsimshian houses and were probably the prototype for the carved interior central poles favoured by many Haida chiefs. Their placement at the centre of the house under the peak of the roof allowed them to be up to 5.5 m (18 feet) tall, as in Chief Skidegate's house. The carved interior central pole was usually a complicated sculpture based on a founding myth of the family. Amos Russ and Tom Stevens, two chiefs of Skidegate, provided John R. Swanton (1905:129) with different interpretations of a nineteenth-century pole carved by Charles Edenshaw. Boas (1927:209-12) comments on the variability of interpretation as follows:

> Swanton . . . had two informants; both explained the top figure as an eagle but they differed
> as to the meaning of the rest. The one claimed that the lower part of the pole represented the
> story of a woman being carried away by a killer-whale. The woman's face shows just below
> the eagle's beak, and the whale's blow-hole is represented by a small face above the face of the

PLATE 85

From stylistic evidence, this Sea Lion house post (one of a pair), 9 feet (2.7 m) high, came from an old house in Howkan village in Alaska. They appear to have been repainted by a native artist just before they were sold. *Acquired by George T. Emmons for the Lord Bossom collection.* CMC VII-B-1810A, (S94-6760)

killer-whale. The second informant, however, explained the large face at the bottom as that of a grizzly bear, presumably meaning thereby the sea-grizzly bear; and the small figure over it as the "sea ghost" which usually rides upon its back. The woman's face he left unexplained. . . . Obviously in this case the symbolism is not clear enough to enable an Indian who does not know the artist or who does not know the meaning of the carving to interpret it correctly.

One exquisite house model from Masset is a relatively authentic portrayal of Chief Wiah's Na Yuans (or Monster House), carved for Indian agent Thomas Deasey (PLATE 135). As the historical photos show, that house did indeed have carved corner posts, as well as a large frontal pole depicting the flood story of Qingi, whose large bearlike figure sits atop both the model pole and the real pole (PLATE 136). The Eagle, a crest of Wiah's, takes flight from Qingi's head in both versions. A standing Beaver interior pole is also depicted.

The actual interior central pole from Chief Wiah's Monster House now stands in front of the Haida house in the Grand Hall of the Canadian Museum of Civilization (PLATE 86). It portrays a standing Beaver gnawing a stick inlaid with about a hundred pieces of abalone shell. The nostrils of the Beaver also have abalone inlay, and its paws and tail have small faces on them. On its head are six *skil-daden* (or potlatch rings), a feature frequently associated with the Beaver. A similar carving stood outside of Wiah's house but sported a much larger stack of nine potlatch rings. Both versions, the one for external display and the other for display inside the house, were undoubtedly created by the same artist. The Beaver crest was given to Chief Wiah by Chief Legaic of Fort Simpson, who had a similar pole with thirteen potlatch rings standing in front of his house. The crest's origin goes back to the supernatural beavers who lived at Kitselas Canyon on the Skeena River.

On both versions of the pole, there is a large face that appears to consist of a series of six sculpted bands, which I now believe represents the segmented body of a Dragonfly, although I earlier identified it as a Sculpin (MacDonald 1983:143). The two crests are often portrayed as alternates of each other. This truly remarkable sculpture is the only item that was saved from Monster House, the largest dwelling on Haida Gwaii, thanks to the prompt efforts of Charles F. Newcombe as the house and poles were being cut up and burned early this century.

Interior Screens, Housepits and Smokeholes

Few examples survive of the Haida decorated screen that stood between the rear house posts, comparable to the spectacular interior screens of their Tsimshian and Tlingit neighbours. These wall partitions could be assembled in front of the chief's compartment to conceal dancers as they put on their costumes and prepared to perform. Access to the public area was through a round or oval doorway that formed part of an ancestral or crest figure painted on the screen.

One model of a house from Kiusta village, made by Charles Edenshaw for John R. Swanton, has a doorway in the mouth of a froglike design (said to represent Konankada) on

PLATE 86

An interior house pole of
Chief Wiah (*right*), displaying
his crest of a standing Beaver
with a Dragonfly on its belly.
The Beaver is gnawing a stick
inlaid with nearly one hundred
pieces of abalone shell. This
pole was probably carved
when the house was
constructed circa 1850. It now
stands before the Haida house
in the Grand Hall of the
Canadian Museum of
Civilization. *Acquired from
Chief Henry Wiah of Masset in
1901 by Charles F. Newcombe.*
CMC VII-B-1130 (S92-4407)

PLATE 87

An argillite model of a house
in which the figures at the
ends of the rafters portray
singers who perform when
anyone approaches. The
housefront is decorated with
the image of a Grizzly Bear.
*Acquired on Haida Gwaii
(probably Skidegate) circa 1892
by James Deans for the A.
Aaronson collection.* CMC VII-B-
816 (S92-4274)

the screen (Swanton 1905:fig. 6). The most spectacular surviving Haida screen is from How-kan village in Alaska (PLATE 149). George T. Emmons, who collected this piece, identifies its images in his unpublished notes (no date) but does not identify the house from which it came.

Other features of the Haida house that were sometimes elaborated with carving or paint-ing were the rafters (PLATE 87), the retaining planks that framed the housepit surrounding the central fireplace, and the timbers around the smokehole above the fireplace. No carved housepit planks survive for the Haida (though there are Tlingit and Tsimshian examples), but the most elaborate of all known examples from anywhere on the coast belonged to Charles Edenshaw's son Henry in the village of Klinkwan, Alaska (PLATE 142). The design is composed of elaborately carved and painted chests (with opercula shell inlay) that alternate with engraved coppers. Although Henry Edenshaw inherited this house, it was probably built by Albert Edward Edenshaw, who may have commissioned his nephew Charles Eden-shaw to create this design.

The smokehole had mythical significance among the Haida, as it was the opening through which souls entered and left the house at birth and death, following the pathway of smoke uniting this world to the upper world and the Milky Way, which was the pathway of souls in the sky. It was also the opening through which the trickster-hero Raven escaped to carry his gifts of the sun, the moon and the stars to humans. It was while flying through this opening that the White Raven, the primal form, turned black in the smoke.

One notable smokehole carving depicts a double-headed Killer Whale with prominent dorsal fins (PLATE 88). In form, it resembles the double-headed soul catchers traditionally used by Tsimshian shaman but on occasion by Haida shaman as well. The placement of a soul catcher as a device to protect souls in the smokehole of a house presents some intriguing equations in the cycles of birth and death.

FURNISHINGS

Haida houses had little in the way of furnishings in the European sense. Sleeping compart-ments and privacy were provided by plank partitions that were often elaborately decorated. During ceremonies, additional screens were added to the back of the house to create a back-stage area for dancers and initiates to put on their costumes. These screens were often made of canvas obtained in trade and were painted with crest designs. Storage boxes were stacked around the sides of the house. Formal seats were reserved for the chief and his wives, while others sat on boxes or on mats on the floor.

The chief's seat of honour in each house was located along the back platform on the cen-tral axis of the house, facing the door. The seat was thought of as a box that protected the spirit of the chief. Hence, the decoration is typically either the Konankada design or a crest belonging to the chief (PLATE 114). The decoration on a chief's seat is on the inside, so the seated chief was shown to public view surrounded by his carved and painted crests.

PLATE 88

A small human figure crouches between two Killer Whales on this protective device made in the form of a shaman's soul catcher. It may have been placed in the smokehole of a house to prevent the souls of its inhabitants from wandering away during illness. The painted details are Tsimshian in style, but the piece is recorded as Haida in the catalogue of the Lord Bossom collection. *Acquired by George T. Emmons before 1900 for the Lord Bossom collection.* CMC VII-B-1821 (S92-4385)

117

Boxes and Chests

Boxes were used to store food stuffs, clothing, regalia and ritual paraphernalia such as rattles and whistles. Some boxes were simply made of bent sheets of cedar bark sewn at the corners and base to provide disposable containers for trade items, while others were more substantial and durable bentwood boxes. Bentwood boxes for food (PLATE 89) ranged in capacity from a couple of litres (quarts) up to 225 L (50 gallons). George M. Dawson (in Cole and Lockner 1989:475) observed that boxes of eulachon grease brought to the islands for trade by the Tsimshian required two men each to pack them up the beach from the canoes.

Bentwood storage boxes destined to store important wealth objects were provided with a guardian spirit decoration in the form of supernatural marine beings and more familiar animals (PLATES 90, 91). They also had heavy plank lids, whose edges were decorated with vertical rows of opercula shells. For transport, the lids were tied in place with elaborate knotwork of cedar bark cordage (PLATE 91).

The design field of a bentwood box has provided a constant challenge for art historians and native scholars alike to interpret. Although the design is standard, the variations are endless and intriguing. The "front" of the box normally depicts Konankada (the Chief of the Undersea World), with fins as well as human hands. The face has double-eye forms (two salmon heads joined at the nose). The "back" of the box is a variation of this creature with single-pupil eyes. This supernatural being may be modified by the addition of such markers as large incisors (Beaver), gill slits (Dogfish), large canines (Wolf), tall ears and protruding tongue (Bear), and so on. The side panels of the box have much simpler designs, which are only painted and not carved.

A variation of the standard box design is to spread the traditional front and back image of the supernatural being over the two sides, so that its protective power is continuous around the box.

Some box designs defy a simple analysis. They do not relate to a supernatural guardian figure but use multiple elements, including human faces manipulated freely. Franz Boas (1955:fig. 287) challenged Charles Edenshaw to provide an interpretation for such a box, which is now in the collection of the American Museum of Natural History in New York City. Edenshaw provided an explanation of each panel as part of a Raven myth, but few others have been able to comprehend the shorthand interpretation of the visual symbolism he provided. Bill Reid refers to this box as "the final exam" in understanding Northwest Coast art. Few manage to pass that exam.

Large bentwood chests, approximately the size of two storage boxes, were favoured by chiefs to store and protect their regalia, particularly their costumes of Chilkat or button blankets, aprons, leggings and frontlets. Important chiefs owned up to half a dozen such chests (PLATES 5, 92, 94). The major centres of production for these chests throughout the nineteenth century were at Bella Bella and Fort Simpson. Since Fort Simpson was viewed by all the tribes of the north coast as the hub of trade for expensive goods, including high-quality items of native manufacture, and also had the largest cadre of professional artists throughout the last two-thirds of the nineteenth century, it was probably the source of chests acquired by the Haida, who visited the post annually.

PLATE 89

Food storage boxes were usually not decorated, but occasionally one such as this example was painted with the image of the supreme Chief of the Seas, the being ultimately responsible for all of the other sea creatures that the Haida used for food. Their flesh was under its guardianship while in such a box, which in turn honoured that supernatural being. *Collected at Masset circa 1895 by Charles F. Newcombe.* CMC VII-B-324 (S92-4198)

118

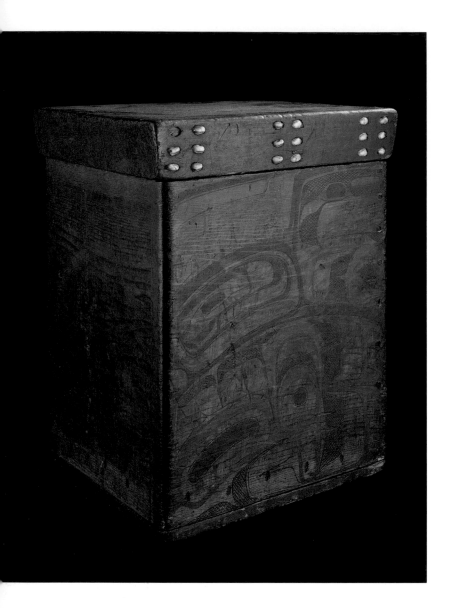

PLATE 90A, 90B, 90C, 90D

The unusual decoration on all four sides of this bentwood storage box displays the idiosyncratic style practised by some Skidegate Inlet artists towards the end of the nineteenth century. *From the Lord Bossom collection.* CMC VII-X-621 (S94-6786/6787/6788/6789)

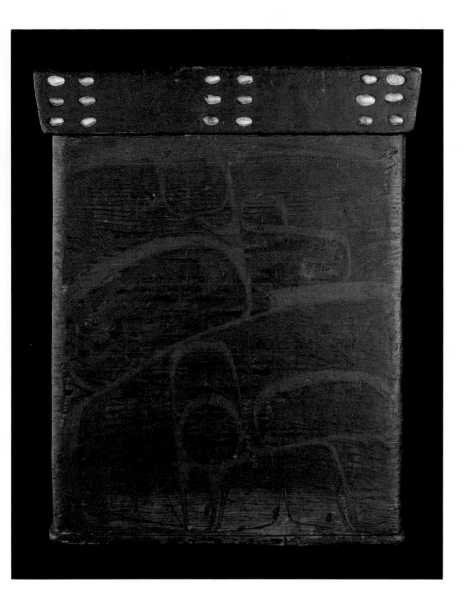
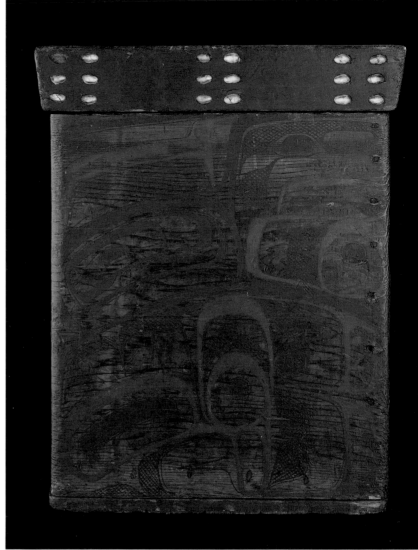

PLATE 93A, 93B, 93C
This exquisite bentwood burial chest is one of the finest in the collection of the Canadian Museum of Civilization. On the front panel (*facing page*), the hands are inlaid with separately carved faces. At each corner, the salmon trout head ovoids indicate the work of an exquisite craftsman. The circles around the eyes of the human face in the lower centre of the panel are the signature feature of an unknown artist whose work was widely traded on the north coast in the mid-nineteenth century. The front, back and one side are shown here. *Collected at Skedans in 1932 by Robert Bruce Inverarity.* CMC VII-B-1881 (s92-4379 front, s92-4381 back, s92-4382 left)

The design of the standard chest uses the face of the double-eyed supernatural being on the front panel, while the back portrays the single-eyed being. The sides are often decorated with simple formlines and ovoids, but on a series of chests that were probably imported to Haida Gwaii, the side panels have full designs that resemble the fronts of storage boxes.

After protecting the wealth of a chief during his lifetime, such a chest often became his burial box and the protector of his soul after death (PLATES 93, 95, 96, 105, 111, 120).

Basketry

Haida women made a range of baskets from large coarsely woven ones that would allow clams to drain, to drinking cups so tightly woven they would hold water. Every woman had her work baskets, which were usually hung from the walls or rafters of the house. Other baskets were made for the storage of clothes, as well as roots and vegetables. Cooking baskets of red cedar bark with an open weave were used to boil berries, prior to mashing and drying them for winter use. Woven strainers were used to skim off the grease when boiling black cod. Potato baskets became a common item when, as part of the nineteenth-century economy, the Haida grew potatoes to sell to mainland natives and maritime traders.

Containers were also woven for a great many other specific functions such as burden baskets, bait baskets, basket quivers for arrows and even stout baskets for anchor stones. Cradles were also fashioned of basketry, although wooden ones were more popular. Fancy baskets for storing soapberry spoons became something of a specialty, as did drinking cups, and very fine examples were woven for domestic use as well as for trade.

Women also wove many types of basketry mats for household use. Meals were eaten on them, babies were born on them, people slept on them and the dead were wrapped in them for burial. Old mats were recycled as covers for boxes or for covering canoes to keep them from checking in the sunlight. Designs on mats were geometric but could be quite complex. Some patterns had individual names and meanings, and specific designs belonged as a privilege to certain families of high rank. These design motifs have not been thoroughly analysed, but in his unpublished notes, Charles F. Newcombe (1902:MS) documented the names of many of them, such as "slug trail," "comb pattern," "shadow," "small waves in calm waters," "the crossing of the sticks of a drying frame for fish," "little breeze on the water" and so on. Museum collections contain numerous painted mats, some of which may be attributed to the Haida, but many appear to be intended for the early tourist trade and there is no evidence they were ever produced in Haida country.

Although the art of weaving hats, mats and baskets almost disappeared from the 1930s until the late 1950s, the recent renaissance of feasting has encouraged young women to learn basketry from their grandmothers. Dorothy Grant from Hydaburg, Alaska, typifies the younger generation who have mastered this skill, and she has produced a wide range of hats and baskets. The Haida artist Robert Davidson has painted crest designs on many pieces of her work, including hats. These new pieces are as fine as any old examples and are sought after by museums in North America and Japan.

PLATE 94

One of the painted end panels of a large bentwood chest. This particular style of chest with carved front and back panels, as well as elaborately painted end panels, was produced by specialized craftsmen at Bella Bella and Fort Simpson. *Collected at Masset in 1898 by Charles F. Newcombe.* CMC VII-B-457.2 (S92-4203)

127

PLATE 95

The back of a bentwood burial chest that has both painted and incised formline designs wrapping around two sides. The ovoids are extremely thick at the top, and the inner ovoids have simple slits indicating closed eyes. Such chests were often found in burial caves, although this example was never used. *Acquired by Charles F. Newcombe in 1898.* CMC VII-B-1559 (S92-4311)

128

PLATE 96

On this bentwood burial chest, the face of the Beaver crest projects from the front in high relief. It was created,
according to Wilson Duff (personal communication) by Charles Edenshaw during his residence at Port Essington at the
mouth of the Skeena. Its form bears a striking resemblance to the sculpted facade of Grizzly Bear's Mouth House at
Skidegate, where Edenshaw grew up. Here, however, the design is totally rearranged to be displayed entirely on the front
panel rather than being wrapped around all four sides in the usual fashion, a further indication that it was a burial chest
meant to be seen only from one perspective. The artist may have intended to use it for his own funeral, but he sold it to
another chief instead. *Collected by Harlan I. Smith in 1926 from a chief at the Gitksan village of Kitwanga on the Skeena
River.* CMC VII-C-1183 (K84-274)

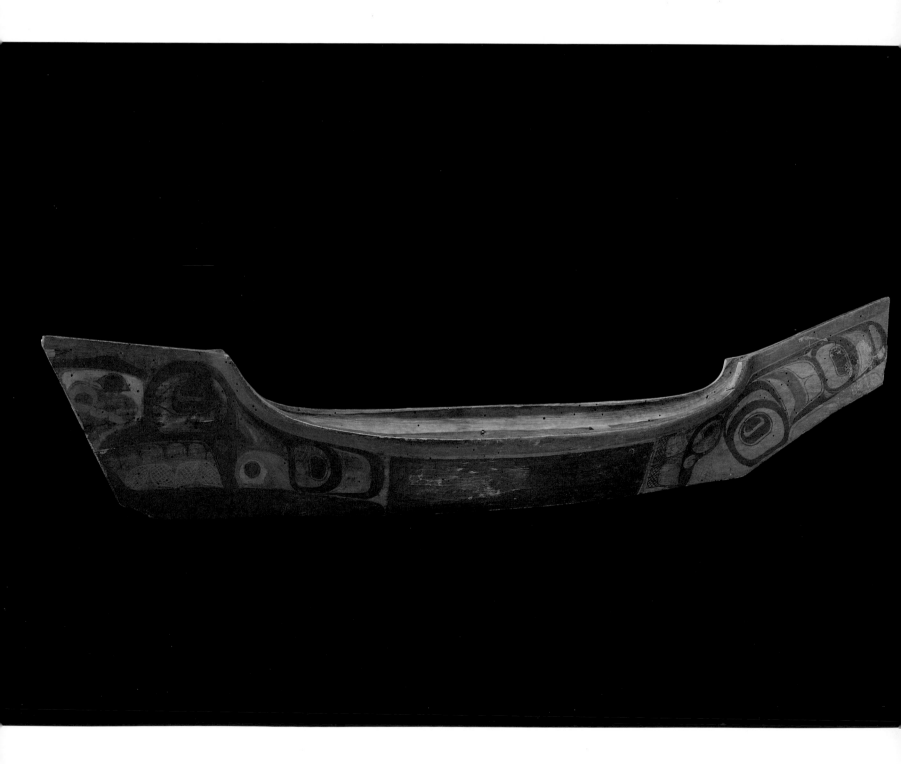

CANOES AND TRADE

PLATE 97

A model of an ancient style of war canoe, often called a "head canoe," whose broad prow was designed to display the crests of the chief who owned it. This type of canoe had disappeared from use by the middle of the nineteenth century, although models were still made after that date. *Collected on Haida Gwaii (probably at Masset) before 1892 by Edward Harris, a Hudson's Bay Company fur trader.* CMC VII-X-280 (S94-6773)

Haida canoes were exquisite craft hewn from the gigantic red cedar that grows on Haida Gwaii and were highly prized by chiefs of other nations throughout the coast. The combination of beautiful lines that pleased the most demanding navigator with the fine craftsmanship and the superior quality of the cedar available on Haida Gwaii literally made Haida canoes the Cadillacs of the coast.

Canoemakers in each village worked on their new craft throughout the autumn at sites where the very best red cedars stood. After an appropriate snowfall that facilitated sledding, the roughed-out canoes were moved from the woods to the nearest beach and towed to the home village, where they were finished over the winter. In the spring, lightly manned flotillas of new canoes left Skidegate Inlet, Masset and Rose Spit on the north coast, braving the seasonal storms to head for the mainland. If these vessels could withstand a crossing of the treacherous Hecate Strait, they could withstand any weather the coast could provide. At the Nass River, the canoes were traded to coastal tribes assembled to take advantage of the spring eulachon fishery. Old canoes were taken in trade by the Haida for their return journey home.

When the first Europeans arrived, they made drawings depicting the Haida in their large war canoes with high prows emblazoned with the crests of the owners. Although there are many models of these canoes, called "head canoes," no full-sized ones have been preserved.

By the end of the eighteenth century, the Haida had learned from visiting sailors and sea captains how to rig sails, and thereafter most large canoes were fitted with two or three masts and sails of canvas or cedar bark mats. These faster, more manoeuvrable craft were capable of carrying 20 000 kg (10 tons) of freight.

The development of this new craft was probably responsible for the disappearance of the "head" type of canoe. The head canoe had a massive prow extending far in front, which was ideal for bearing the crests of the war chief but was a detriment to manoeuvrability under sail. Models of head canoes continued to be made until they began to fade in the memories of carvers (PLATE 97).

War canoes had the same sharp projecting prow as the freight canoes but, in addition to the two-dimensional painted designs on the hull, they often had separate carved crests at the prow or stern (PLATE 98). A stunning example of this style of war canoe was made by Alfred Davidson and other master canoemakers (including Robert Davidson Sr., Robert Davidson's

grandfather) for a world's fair in the United States (PLATES 99, 100). The paintings on it were designed and executed by Charles Edenshaw. When the final price proved too high for the fair's budget, the craft was purchased for the Canadian Museum of Civilization. At 17 m (56 feet) in length, this is the largest Haida war canoe that has survived (although the Heiltsuk war canoe at the American Museum of Natural History in New York is considerably longer).

In 1985, Bill Reid was commissioned to make a 15-m (50-foot) dugout canoe for Expo 86, the world's fair in Vancouver. This beautiful craft he called *Lootas* (or *Wave Eater*). After the fair, several replicas were made in fiberglass, the first two of which were for the Canadian Museum of Civilization. The original canoe was taken to France and paddled up the Seine to Paris, in honour of the bicentennial of the French Revolution. Later, it undertook a much-publicized voyage from Vancouver to Haida Gwaii and has since been kept at Skidegate for ceremonial occasions.

WARFARE

The Haida were feared along the coast because of their practice of making lightning raids against which their enemies had little defence. Their great skills of seamanship, their superior craft and their relative protection from retaliation in their island fortress added to the aggressive posture of the Haida towards neighbouring tribes. Diamond Jenness, an early anthropologist at the Canadian Museum of Civilization, caught their essence in his description of the Haida as the "Indian Vikings of the North West Coast" (1934:243):

> Those were stirring times, about a century ago, when the big Haida war canoes, each hollowed out of a single cedar tree and manned by fifty or sixty warriors, traded and raided up and down the coast from Sitka in the north to the delta of the Fraser River in the south. Each usually carried a shaman or medicine man to catch and destroy the souls of enemies before an impending battle; and the women who sometimes accompanied the warriors fought as savagely as their husbands.

The Haida went to war to acquire objects of wealth, such as coppers and Chilkat blankets, that were in short supply on the islands, but primarily for slaves, who enhanced their productivity or were traded to other tribes. High-ranking captives were also the source of other property received in ransom such as crest designs, dances and songs.

Even prehistorically, the Haida engaged in sea battles. They tied cedar bark ropes to heavy stone rings that were hurled to smash enemy canoes and that could quickly be retrieved for subsequent throws. A stone weighing 18 to 23 kg (40 to 50 pounds) could shatter the side of a dugout canoe and cause it to founder. Most tribes avoided sea battles with the Haida and tried to lure them ashore for a more equitable fight. The Tsimshian developed a signal-fire system to alert their villages on the Skeena River as soon as Haida invaders reached the mainland (MacDonald, no date).

PLATE 98

A Bear crest from the prow of a Haida war canoe. Such figures were added for ceremonial occasions and removed when the canoe had to be stripped for battle. *Collected on Haida Gwaii in 1879 by Israel W. Powell.* CMC VII-B-1054 (S92-4297)

PLATE 99

The only surviving Haida war canoe, 17 m (56 feet) in length with a beam of nearly 2 m (6 feet). It was commissioned for the 1904 American world's fair from Alfred Davidson and other Masset carvers, including Robert Davidson Sr. The original paddles were lost en route to Ottawa, but Charles Edenshaw made a replacement set. *Collected at Masset in 1908 by Reverend William Hogan and R. W. Brock.* CMC VII-B-1128 (S92-4299)

134

PLATE 100

Alfred Davidson of Masset, shown carving the canoe that was commissioned for the 1904 American world's fair. It was painted with Sea Wolf designs by Charles Edenshaw and is now on display at the Canadian Museum of Civilization (PLATE 99). *Photograph by Edward Sapir, 1914.* CMC 26665

The florescence of warfare was undoubtedly accelerated in the half century from 1780 to 1830, when the Haida had no effective enemies except the many European and American traders on their shores who would rather trade than fight. During this period, the Haida successfully captured more than half a dozen ships. One was the ship *Eleanora,* taken by chiefs of the village of Skungwai (or Ninstints) in retaliation for the maltreatment Chief Koyah had received from its captain (MacDonald 1983:46). An even more spectacular event was the capture of the ship *Susan Sturgis* by Chief Wiah of Masset and the rescue of its crew by Albert Edward Edenshaw. In such conflicts, the Haida quickly learned the newcomers' fighting tactics, which they used to good effect in subsequent battles (Brink 1974:38):

> As early as 1795, a British trading ship fired its cannons at a village in the central part of the archipelago because some of the crew had been killed by the inhabitants, and the survivors had to put hastily to sea when the Indians fired back at them. They found out later that the Indians had used a cannon and ammunition pilfered from an American Schooner a few years earlier.

Swivel guns were added to many Haida war canoes, although initially the recoil on discharge caused the hulls of many craft to split.

Fortified sites were part of the defensive strategy of all Northwest Coast groups for at least 2,000 years. Captain George Dixon (Dixon 1789) was so impressed with one Haida fort off the west coast of Graham Island that he called it Hippah Island after the Maori forts he had seen in New Zealand. Military defences at Haida forts included stout palisades, rolling top-log defences, heavy trapdoors and fighting platforms supplied with stores of large boulders to hurl at invaders.

Warriors wore various kinds of armour including war helmets (PLATE 101), wooden visors to protect their necks, and breastplates that were often concealed under a leather tunic emblazoned with their crests. Few Haida wooden slat breastplates have survived, although numerous Tlingit examples exist in museums. There are, however, many Haida painted leather tunics.

Haida body armour favoured the war coat, which was made of the thick hides of sea lions (PLATE 102) or of several layers of elkskin. The former was available through trade on the Nass River while the latter was acquired from European and American traders who obtained them from tribes at the mouth of the Columbia River.

The Haida replaced the bow and arrow and short spear with firearms as soon as they became available early in the nineteenth century, and some proud owners carved their crests onto the stocks of their muskets. War daggers, however, continued to be used in close combat, and many hundreds of them have been collected from northern tribes. These daggers became something of an art form in themselves and were treasured for many generations within the families of chiefs. The descendants of the famous Tsimshian Chief Legaic kept his war dagger until the 1980s, when its value had climbed to over a hundred thousand dollars.

By the 1830s, endemic warfare had given way to the Pax Britannica on the Northwest Coast, as warfare became too costly for the land-based fur traders to tolerate. John R. Swanton was struck by the similarity between war and potlatching among the Haida (1905:155): "Feasts . . . and the potlatches were the Haida roads to greatness more than war. The latter, when not waged to avenge injuries, was simply a means of increasing their power to give the former."

PLATE 102

The full outfit of a north coast warrior: a round wooden helmet, a bentwood visor, and a painted leather tunic over a breastplate made of interlocking wooden slats. This type of armour had its origins in the bronze age of China and Japan. Its use in the New World was limited to the west coast, but elements of the outfit, particularly wooden slat breastplates, spread as far south as California. CMC VII-X-1073 (S94-13,386)

HAIDA GWAII

Today, most of the Haida population in Canada lives on Haida Gwaii, particularly Graham Island, but in prehistoric times they were much more evenly distributed throughout the archipelago. According to the early fur traders, there were concentrations of population in the south at Skungwai (or Ninstints) village and in the north at Cloak Bay, where there was a cluster of villages, including Kiusta, Dadens and Yaku. On the north coast, on Masset Inlet, there were the major villages of Masset, Yan and Kayung; and on Skidegate Inlet, there was the village of Skidegate. The locations chosen for these settlements protected them from the winter storms that lash the Pacific coast and Hecate Strait.

Although the Haida spent most of the year in their sizable towns, during the fishing season they dispersed to every stream or river that had a fish run. Salmon were the primary food species, although they run only on alternate years on Haida Gwaii. All Haida had access to the rich halibut fishing grounds, and villages on the west coast relied heavily on black cod. Shellfish was readily available, except on the west coast. Eulachon, a variety of herring rich in oil, was not indigenous to on Haida Gwaii, so the Haida travelled to the huge runs on the Nass River on the mainland, where they traded for other foods and rare materials that were not available in their homeland.

A late visitor to Haida Gwaii, Newton H. Chittenden (1884:75), who went to the villages of Cumshewa, Skedans, Tanu and Skungwai as part of a survey for the British Columbia government, reported:

> All the villages named are beautifully situated, facing the south from cosy sheltered nooks, with splendid beaches, and abundant supplies of food conveniently near. Besides the halibut bank marked on the chart, there is one near all of the villages mentioned, and inexhaustible quantities of clams and mussels along the neighbouring shores. This is certainly one of the most favoured regions in the world for the abode of the Indian.

Skungwai (Ninstints)

Ninstints, the name under which this village was declared a World Heritage Site by UNESCO in 1983, is also the name of the town chief in the middle of the last century (PLATE 103). An

PLATE 103

A portrait of Chief Ninstints (Tom Price, *left*) and Chief Giatlins (John Robson, *right*). Tom Price (circa 1860–1927) was the last traditional chief of Ninstints (Skungwai) to live in the village and was also a talented carver of argillite. John Robson, a famous carver, was the successor to Chief Giatlins and stepfather of Charles Edenshaw. *Studio portrait by an unknown Victoria photographer circa 1884.*

earlier town chief in the late eighteenth century whose name was Koyah (Work in Dawson 1880:173B) had his attack on a trading ship immortalized in a folk song popular among New England whalers (Howay 1929:15):

Come all ye bold Northwestmen who plough the raging main,
Come listen to my story, while I relate the same;
'Twas of the *Lady Washington* decoyed as she lay,
At Queen Charlotte's Island, in North America.

On the sixteenth day of June, boys, in the year Ninety-One,
The natives in great numbers on board our ship did come,
Then for to buy our fur of them our captain did begin,
But mark what they attempted before long time had been.

The Haida name of Skungwai (or Red Snapper Island Town) refers to the small island behind which the village shelters. The island on which the village sits is called Kunghit (or Anthony) Island. Skungwai has taken on a symbolic status today, primarily because its remote location helped to preserve more *in situ* totem poles there than in any other Haida village. Two tragedies, however, claimed some of the beautiful poles from Skungwai. The first was a fire in the last century, which burned one end of the village and half a dozen poles; it was supposedly set by the Heiltsuk people in retaliation for a raid. The second was another fire, which destroyed the workshop of the Queen Charlotte Islands Museum at Skidegate, where seven poles from Skungwai had been sent for restoration. These lost poles were part of a collection of more than a dozen of the finest poles from Skungwai that had been taken to the Royal British Columbia Museum in Victoria by a salvage expedition in 1957 under the leadership of Professor Harry Hawthorn, Professor Wilson Duff, Michael Kew and Bill Reid. The museum lent some of the poles to the University of British Columbia Museum of Anthropology, where they are still located, and returned the remaining seven to Skidegate, only to meet the tragic end already described.

About a dozen poles still stand at Skungwai, all mortuary posts, now missing their frontal boards (PLATES 104, 105). The bones and objects they once held, such as coppers and labrets (PLATE 106), were scattered or stolen by enthusiastic collectors over the course of more than a century.

Tanu

Tanu, which is located on Laskeek Bay, is an important Haida village whose name refers to a type of sea grass found nearby. It was often called Kloo's village (also spelled Clue or Klue), meaning "southeast (wind)," after the name of its town chief. The town was founded sometime after 1725 and abandoned in the 1880s. The last chief, Gitkun, died in Skidegate early this century.

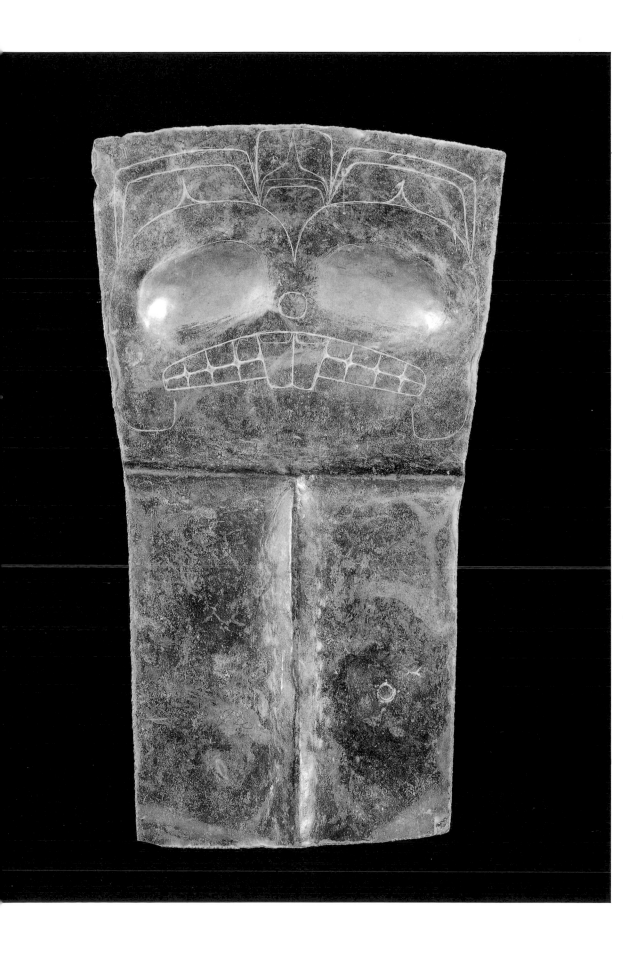

PLATE 105

The front of a chief's burial chest from Skungwai (Ninstints), made in the style of the early nineteenth century. The central figure of a Bear is in high relief and once had abalone shell inlay in the eyes, ears, hands and knees. The bas-relief carvings on the flanking panels were also once inlaid with abalone shell. *Collected at Skungwai (Ninstints) in 1897 by Charles F. Newcombe.*

PLATE 106

From Skungwai (Ninstints) village, a small copper shield depicting a Beaver. The protruding eyes on this figure appear to have been reworked from the original heavily oxidized metal but were not engraved with the expected salmon-head eye designs. *Collected at Skungwai (Ninstints) in 1897 by Charles F. Newcombe.* CMC VII-B-377 (s94-6769)

In 1967, I recorded (but did not excavate) a mass grave at Tanu that represented the last mortuary ceremony performed about 1885, just before the remaining occupants left their village to the encroaching forest. Prompted by the missionaries to inter their dead, the people of Tanu collected all of the remains from the mortuaries and laid them in a common grave of more than fifty individuals (MacDonald and Cybulski 1973:60–113).

George M. Dawson (1880:169B), who visited this village in 1878 during his work for the Canadian Geographical Survey, wrote a vivid description of a Haida house:

> The village consists of perhaps twelve or fourteen of the large houses usual on the coast, & bristles with totem poles carved into Grotesque figures. Some of the houses entered through holes in the bases of the poles, but Clue's by an ordinary door. Descending some steps one is in a rectangular area depressed somewhat below the level of the ground outside, with several broad steps running round it, on which the family goods, bedding &c. placed. In the Centre a square area not boarded in which a bright fire of small logs burns, the smoke passing off through apertures in the roof above. Clue with some of his friends occupied positions on the further side of the fire from the door. Squatting on Clean mats, several women, who however kept in the background.

Dawson went on to add (1880:169B): "There are about 32 upright totem poles in the village of all ages, heights, & styles . . . about sixteen, including one unfinished, though evidently some time under way." He was also fortunate enough to witness the raising of a totem pole, which he describes (1880:169B):

> There were a considerable number of strangers here at the time of our visit in July, 1878, engaged in the erection of a carved post and house for the chief. The nights are given to dancing, while sleep and gambling divided the portions of the day which were not employed in the business at hand. Cedar planks of great size, hewn out long ago in anticipation, had been towed to the spot, and were now being dragged up the beach by the united efforts of the throng, dressed for the most part in gaily coloured blankets. They harnessed themselves in clusters to the ropes, as the Egyptians are represented to have done in their pictures, shouting and ye-hooing in strange tones to encourage themselves in the work.

Dawson also took a photograph of Tanu (PLATE 107): "Present Chief Klue with a pound of tobacco, & finding no objection take a photo of the village. Would have taken several but the rain threatening all the morning now began." The photograph is the only one that portrays Haida village life of the time as it might have been observed on a casual visit. At least a dozen people appear in the photo, including a totem pole carver at work, not to mention several dogs. Domestic enterprises are evident in clothing hung to air next to a rain barrel, and halibut fillets and other foodstuffs drying on a rack. The greatest activity occurs at the door to Chief Gitkun's house, beside a double row of food boxes covered with cedar bark

PLATE 107

The village of Tanu in July 1878. George M. Dawson (1880:169B) notes that the community was undergoing a succession of town chiefs; a trading party of Tsimshian, gathered before the entrance of the town chief's house, were gambling as they waited for the raising of the new chief's pole, to which the carver is shown applying the finishing touches. *Photograph by George M. Dawson. National Archives of Canada* 242

mats and tied neatly with cords for a sea journey.

James G. Swan visited Tanu in 1883, just five years after Dawson. He was accompanied by Chief Gitkun's son Kitkune, who volunteered to show him his father's great house (Lucile McDonald 1972: 190–91):

> He entered it by knocking off one of the massive planks, crawled inside and unfastened the door so that Swan's party could bring their cargo kit inside . . . The place was of huge proportions, fifty feet [15 m] long and with walls eight inches [20 cm]thick. Young Kitkune opened a hidden door and revealed a chamber where sacred emblems of the old chief were kept. The owner was reluctant to part with many and then only for a large price.

Swan (1883:Sept. 18) notes in his diary: "I would have been willing to pass several days at Laskeek [Tanu] as there is more of interest there than at any village I have seen." He wanted to experience as much as possible and persuaded Kitkune to show him more (McDonald 1972:191): "Young Kitkune took Swan to an uncle's tomb, a small structure behind the big house. The sepulchre contained an elaborately carved box, two guns, ammunition boxes, and the carved stick the dead man had held when distributing presents at potlatches."

For the Columbian World Exposition in Chicago in 1893, Swan collected an exceptional interior central pole about 5 m (16 feet) high, which stood in Easy to Enter House (PLATE 108, 109). The crests on it belong to the chief's wife, who claimed rights to the crests of the chief of Skedans village. After the fair, the pole was deposited in the Field Museum, which sold the pole but kept a unique talking stick (shaped like a narwhal tusk and inlaid with abalone shell) that was attached to it. The pole went through several private owners before it was purchased by the Canadian Museum of Civilization. The Field Museum kindly restored the talking stick to the pole, where it now protrudes prominently from the forehead of the lowest of two Wasgo (or Sea Wolf) figures. The myth associated with this pole is that of the Wasgo, who lived in the lake behind Skidegate village and had the ability to transform between the form of a Wolf and a Killer Whale. The pole shows the Wasgo in two states, with and without his Whale attributes. According to Bill Holm, the pole was carved by the unnamed artist whom he has dubbed "the Master of the Chicago Settee." Several of the house frontal poles collected by Swan for the exposition passed through various owners until they were eventually acquired by the Canadian Museum of Civilization.

At the time of Swan's visit, only fifteen people were living at Tanu. The mortuary columns outnumbered the totem poles and houses of the inhabitants.

PLATE 109

The same interior house pole from Easy to Enter House in Tanu as in PLATE 108, restored and on display in the Grand Hall of the Canadian Museum of Civilization. The narwhal tusk talking stick, which was separated from the pole for a number of years, has been replaced in its original position. CMC VII-B-1797A (pole), CMC VII-B-1797B (talking stick)

Skedans

Skedans village is located on the neck of a peninsula of land at the head of Cumshewa Inlet (PLATE 112). A high rocky prominence at the end of the peninsula offered a perfect site for a fort to protect the village. Skedans is a European rendering of the name of the town chief, Gida'nsta. The Haida name for this town is Koona, or in the old days Huadji-lanas, which means Grizzly Bear Town. Chief Gida'nsta maintained a special relationship with Chief Tsebassa, town chief of the Tsimshian village of Kitkatla opposite Skedans on the mainland. According to a charter myth, both town chiefs had a common ancestor who had migrated from the Nass River (Swanton 1905:79). This alliance provided the main channel through which trade and potlatching took place.

The Haida exchanged their dried halibut, dried seaweed, herring roe and canoes with the Tsimshian for eulachon grease, dried berries, goat wool and horns. Friendly competition in the potlatch system encouraged the exchange of crests, songs and stories, and it appears that the secret society structure of the Nuxalk and other central coast tribes moved from Kitkatla to Skedans via this connection (PLATE 111).

George M. Dawson's recently published field notes provide a much richer insight into Haida life than his official monograph issued a year after the expedition, such as this record of his impression of Skedans during a visit in July 1878 (in Cole and Lockner 1989:473):

> Skedan's village shows signs of having passed its best days some time since, though not quite so deserted as Cumshewa's. It has always been a larger village & many of the houses are still inhabited. Most, however, look old & moss grown & the totem poles have the same aspect. Of houses there are about sixteen, of totem poles about 44. These last seem to be put up not merely as hereditary family Crests, but in memory of the dead . . . The flat topped, boarded totems are more frequent in this village than elsewhere seen. One of these shows a curious figure leaning forward & holding in its paws a genuine *Copper* like those described to me by Mr. Moffat as in great request & much worth among the Ft Rupert Indians. At least one other *Copper* in view on the posts here, but the second observed not in Evident relation to any of the Carved figures.

Dawson (in Cole and Lockner 1989:474) was a keen observer of the routine activities that occupied the community:

> About sundown two large Canoes with two masts Each, & the forward one with a large flag hoisted, hove in sight round the point. Turn out to be Kit-Katla Chimseyan Indians with loads of oolachen grease for Sale. They have slept only two nights on the way from Kit-Katla. They come here on a regular trading expedition, & expect to carry back chiefly blankets in place of their oil . . . Quite a picturesque scene when the Canoes grounded & the Kit-Katlans assisted by the Haidas carry up blankets used as bedding, miscellains little things & the Cedar bark boxes which hold the precious oil.

Cumshewa

PLATE 113A, 113B

(pages 152/153)

A panorama of the village of
Cumshewa in July 1878. Most
of the houses have been
abandoned, and the new
mortuary posts attest to the
deaths of many chiefs in quick
succession. *Photographs by
George M. Dawson.* CMC 244
(left) and 245 (right)

The village of Cumshewa is on the northern shore of Cumshewa Inlet, an hour's paddle from Skedans (PLATE 113). In 1840, the village had about twenty houses and slightly fewer than three hundred inhabitants (Work in Dawson 1880:173B), who belonged to three closely related Eagle lineages.

Cumshewa was an anglicized version of the name of the town chief, Gomshewah, a Heiltsuk word meaning "rich at the mouth of the river." This alludes to the teeming life at a river mouth where seagulls, seals and killer whales congregate to feed upon the salmon that pool there prior to making their spawning run up the river. When the first European ships with their white sails arrived on the coast, the Haida compared them to the flocks of seagulls at spawning time and gave the name Cumshewa to the white people associated with this apparition. The Haida name for the village was Thlinul, anglicized as Tlkinool by John Work (in Dawson 1880:168B), who carried out the first census of the Haida for the Hudson's Bay Company in 1839; the Tsimshian called the village Kit-ta-was.

Joseph Ingraham's journals of 1791 and 1792 (in Kaplanoff 1971:MS 134) record numerous trading activities with Chief Cumshewa and his people, although Ingraham did not leave his ship: "The people of these Isles in generall possess a truly merchantile spirit but none more so than the tribe of Cummashawaa for they will not part with a single skin till they had exerted their utmost to obtain the best price for it."

Reverend Jonathan Green (1915:64), who visited Cumshewa in 1829 when there was a war in progress between that village and the Tsimshian town of Kitkatla, did not leave his ship either:

> We came down opposite Kumshewa village, and several of the Indians came off to see us. This is the tribe, several of whom were killed by the Shebasha men. Some of the sufferers of that quarrel were on board. One lost a child, another a sister, another his wife, besides receiving a wound himself. Their badge of mourning is a face painted horribly black, with their hair cut very short.

George M. Dawson (1880:169) was the first outside visitor to actually enter the village:

> The village generally known as Cumshewas is situated in a small bay facing toward the open sea, but about two miles [3.2 km] within the inlet to which the same name has been applied. The outer point of the bay is formed by a little rock islet, which is connected to the main shore by a beach at low tide . . . There are now standing here twelve or fourteen houses, several of them quite ruinous, with over twenty-five carved posts. The population is quite small, this place having suffered much from the causes to which the decrease in numbers of the natives have already been referred.

Cumshewa was occupied until 1905, when Methodist missionaries encouraged the remaining few inhabitants to move to Skidegate.

154

Kaisun

Kaisun is a village on the west coast of Moresby Island (PLATE II5). It is located at the east end of Inskip Channel, due south of Cha'atl village, with which it has close ties. The town chief of Cha'atl owned a large house in Kaisun, called Dogfish House, which he used when he resided there. Around 1840 there were over three hundred people living in twenty houses in Kaisun (Work in Dawson 1880:173B). All of the inhabitants belonged to an Eagle lineage known as the People of Sea Lion Town.

Skotsgai, the town chief of Kaisun, owned three houses; the principal one was House Upon Which Are Clouds, a Haida equivalent of "skyscraper house." In 1849, the discovery of gold in the area started a short-lived gold rush on the islands. Chief Skotsgai changed his name to Chief Gold, and his town became known as Gold Harbour. A decade later, he moved his villagers to Haina (or New Gold Harbour) near Skidegate on the east side of Haida Gwaii. Charles F. Newcombe purchased several items from Skotsgai, including his beautifully decorated chief's seat (PLATE II4).

The village of Kaisun as it appeared in 1901. The discovery of gold in nearby Mitchell Harbour in 1849 started a gold rush that lasted for a few years and attracted miners from the California rush. *Photograph by Charles F. Newcombe.*

PLATE 116

The frontal pole of House
Waiting for Property (*right*) in
Haina was exhibited at the
Columbian World Exposition
in Chicago in 1893. It has now
been fully restored and stands
in the Grand Hall of the
Canadian Museum of
Civilization. *Photograph by
Richard Maynard, 1884.* CMC
VII-B-1127 (20,529)

Haina (New Gold Harbour)

Haina in Haida means Sunshine Town, and the village is situated at the end of a small island
looking east into the rising sun over Skidegate Bay (PLATE 117). Haina was occupied in the
late 1850s, on a much older site, by the people of Kaisun (Gold Harbour) and Cha'atl villages. Dawson (1880:173B) explains that the reason for the move to Haina was the drastic
decline of population in all the west coast towns due to the introduction of diseases like
smallpox and tuberculosis by the miners in the short-lived gold rush that Chief Gold and his
wife started.

The town chief was Ganai of the Eagle clan, who owned two houses in the village. His
main residence was called House Always Looking for Visitors, and the other was Lightning
House. On the frontal poles of both houses, the main figure wears an immense hat with
alternating light and dark rings, on which sits a Raven. This main figure represents a mythical being who taught the chief the dances of the Dog-Eater Society.

Chief Ganai's main house was distinguished by having two oval entrances on either side
of the frontal pole, as well as by smaller versions of the dog-eater figure or watchmen on the
corner posts. The Raven on the top of the pole ensured that no one overlooked Ganai's
wealth, as it held a large copper in its beak. Although the pole of the main house eventually

PLATE 117

A panorama of the village of Haina (or New Gold Harbour), showing the ten original houses of the chiefs in a row; three more modest dwellings have been added nearer to the beach at left. *Photograph by Richard Maynard, 1884.*

PLATE 118

On this model totem pole, the second figure from the top is that of a shaman holding puffin beak rattles over two patients. *Collected at Haina in 1884 by Alexander McKenzie of the Hudson's Bay Company.* CMC VII-B-842 (S92-4275) fell down and decayed, the pole from Lightning House is now at the Canadian Museum of Civilization.

The pole that stood in front of House Waiting for Property belonged to a Raven lineage, and it is also now at the Canadian Museum of Civilization (PLATE 116). The top figure is a Killer Whale person flanked by two watchmen. The large beak on the figure below belongs to an Eagle crest, and below that is a *tcamaos* (a supernatural snag that devoured canoes) grasping a six-section potlatch cylinder emerging from the head of a Whale.

When I made a very brief test excavation at the edge of one of the house pits at Haina, I found piles of chips of argillite as well as pieces of broken and unfinished argillite carvings. This confirmed various reports that many argillite carvers had lived and worked at Haina, although they may have sold most of their output in Skidegate or Victoria (PLATE 118).

Haina struggled on through the 1880s, and the inhabitants even built a church, but they finally abandoned the town in about 1890.

Cha'atl

Cha'atl is located on Skidegate Inlet and is partly exposed to swells from the open Pacific Ocean (PLATE 119). The shoreline is steep and mostly rocky, with only a few places to draw up large canoes, but the site does enjoy a southern exposure and is far enough up the channel for protection from storms. During the early nineteenth century, the town was a large community: John Work's census (in Dawson 1880:173B) counts 561 people, making it the third-largest community on Haida Gwaii after Masset and Skidegate. The population consisted of both Raven and Eagle families, who lived in about three dozen houses scattered in several rows.

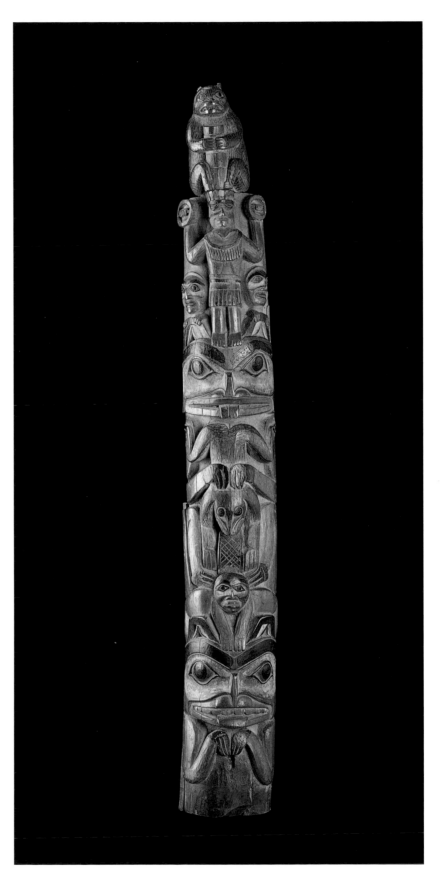

While the location of Cha'atl gave it ideal access to passing trading vessels, the switch in trade after 1834 to the Hudson's Bay Company at Fort Simpson put the town into decline. The town chief of Cha'atl was Wadatstaia, brother of Chief Skotsgai of Kaisun. The discovery of gold on the islands in 1849 led to a gold rush that sustained Cha'atl until the 1860s, when devastating epidemics greatly depopulated the community. The inhabitants began to move to the eastern end of Skidegate Inlet in the 1850s, but Cha'atl was still used by Haida seal hunters until after the turn of the century.

At the end of the nineteenth century, Charles F. Newcombe made a complete photographic and oral history record of Cha'atl and collected many artifacts that are now scattered among museums around the world (PLATE 120). The site was by then heavily overgrown with only four small fish camp houses still habitable. The tangled growth was an extra inducement to the British Columbia artist Emily Carr, who painted one of her most famous Haida scenes from the beach at Cha'atl village.

Although a large fire destroyed part of the town after George M. Dawson's visit in 1878, it is still remarkable today for its well-carved house frontal poles. Unfortunately, none of the magnificent free-standing poles were removed to museums, and today only one, which belonged to the late Solomon Wilson of Skidegate, still survives at the site.

The modern-day village of Skidegate displays little evidence of its creative and tumultuous past. The single exception is the Band Council office building, designed by Rudy Kovaks and enhanced by a pole carved by Bill Reid.

The first contact between Europeans and the people of Skidegate appears to have been made by Captain George Dixon (1789), who in July 1787 anchored off the entrance to Skidegate Inlet. He did not visit the village but does provide the first description of Chief Skidegate:

> Of all the Indians we had seen, this chief had the most savage aspect, and his whole appearance sufficiently marked him as a proper person to lead a tribe of cannibals. His stature was above the common size; his body spare and thin, and though at first sight he appeared lank and emaciated, yet his step was bold and firm, and his limbs apparently strong and muscular.

Dixon's use of the term "cannibals" is an exaggerated reference to the ritual eating of human flesh by the initiates of secret societies. Although in some ceremonies the Tsimshian, Haida and the Kwakw_a_ka'wakw (or Kwakiutl) did bite high-ranking people, it is likely that the Haida only pretended to eat human flesh from cadavers. The care with which they prepared artificial human and dog carcasses in order to fool spectators at the winter dances and initiations is described earlier in this book.

Within a few years of Dixon's visit, many ships included Skidegate in their itinerary while pursuing the trade in sea otter pelts. The name of the town chief was, as usual, applied by the traders to the community itself. Skidegate in Haida means "son of the chiton" (Swanton 1905A:434). One of the best observers is Joseph Ingraham, who recorded his first meeting in 1791 with the town chief of Skidegate in his journal (in Kaplanoff 1971:MS 135–36):

> At 10 oclock in the evening a small canoe was seen coming to us in which was 4 men as she was so small I let them come alongside they said they were of the tribe of Skeetkiss and had furr for sale they sold us but one skin when they could better examine our articles of trade as the least flaw in our chizzles or daggers was sufficient to condemn them as unfit for their purpose . . . Towards night a large war canoe came into the bay and after holding a conversation with some other canoes (perhaps relative to the trade) they came alongside in this canoe was Skeetkiss a chief of the first consequence among these people as at every place we visited they spoke of him as a man of great power and of whom they were afraid.

James Deans, a Hudson's Bay Company employee, describes that chief's successor, who was called Skidegate the Great (1899:77):

> He was named the Great because he was large in body and wealth, if not in good deeds . . . He was a man about six feet in height, had a very small head on an exceedingly large body, so

large that a belt he wore round his waist could go around three ordinary sized men. He was the richest chief of his day. It is said he had thirty slaves, male and female . . . He also had all the neighbouring tribes under his tribute.

Maritime fur traders were cautious about venturing ashore and usually chose to conduct their trade from the relative safety of a well-armed ship. Ingraham (in Kaplanoff 1971:MS 148–49) provides graphic details of the traders' fear of the Haida during his stay in Skidegate Inlet:

> The Evening of the 25 we observed severall war canoes cross the port from Skeetkiss to Cummashawaas village I determin'd to watch them closely for fear of any design upon us therefore doubled our watch severall canoes took up their quarters in the cove about 2 oclock next morning the watch inform'd me the Indians were mustering in the woods as something uncommon was about to take place I order'd all hands immediately and we were soon in readiness to receive them after being on deck about 5 minutes I observed the fires on shore increase and a canoe put off from the beach and paddle towards us a man in her called out to me to look they were going away at the same time they advanced fast towards us I therefore answered him with a swivell and severall musketts on which every fire was immediately extinguished and all silent.

By the 1820s the supply of sea otter furs was beginning to dwindle over much of the north coast, except for Skidegate. In the meantime, the written accounts of maritime traders had begun to interest the mission churches of New England, which had achieved rapid success in Hawaii and were aware of the expanding Russian missions in Alaska. In 1829, Reverend Jonathan Green, who had served the Hawaiian missions, was sent to the Northwest Coast, and provides this description in his journal (1915:84):

> Just before we cast anchor, we passed the village of Skidegas. To me the prospect was almost enchanting, and, more than any thing I had seen, reminded me of a civilized country. The houses, of which there are thirty or forty, appeared tolerably good, and before the door of many of them stood a large mast carved in the form of the human countenance, of the dog, wolf, etc., neatly painted. The land about the village appeared to be in a good state of cultivation. The Indians do not raise much, excepting potatoes, as they have not a variety of seeds; yet, from the appearance of the land, I presume they may greatly vary their vegetable productions.

Reverend Green (1915:85) attempted to preach to the chiefs of Skidegate on board the ship but observed: "When I had finished, they insisted upon my giving them a small drink of rum! . . . On board the ship of a north-west trader is a place very unsuitable to preach temperance to an Indian, and indeed to attempt anything in the form of Christian instructions." He abandoned all plans for a mission at Skidegate.

During the 1830s, whalers began to arrive. In 1832, one whaling captain, a Mr. C. Jefferson, married a daughter of Chief Skidegate the Great and built a residence called Mosquito Hawk House. As he did not own any crests, Jefferson was permitted to use one of his wife's crests, the Raven with a broken beak (a reference to the Raven and the halibut fisherman myth), at the base of his house frontal pole. He filled in the space above the Raven with seven coppers stacked three across as a sign of his wealth.

The fur trade after 1834 swung heavily to the Hudson's Bay Company's new Fort Simpson on the mainland in Tsimshian territory. The Haida from Skidegate visited the fort regularly to trade their potatoes and tobacco to the Tsimshian, who acted as intermediaries.

The discovery of gold in the Queen Charlotte Islands in 1849 brought the first mass influx of whites to the area, but by 1854 the gold rush had subsided. A couple of ships that visited the area in search of gold were wrecked, and James Deans (1899:285) reports that the Skidegate chiefs profited considerably both from the brief gold rush and the ransom of shipwrecked sailors. This windfall led to a flurry of raising new poles and building new houses, but it also gave such a bad reputation to Skidegate that ships stopped calling for a while.

The Haida were bothered by the lack of trading contacts, and in 1853 five hundred of them canoed south to the colonial outposts of Victoria and Nanaimo. Their arrival in Victoria frightened the small settlement, and Governor James Douglas sent them home. However, a few weeks later, a smaller flotilla of five canoes quietly returned to Victoria. This was the beginning of an annual migration that lasted for two decades, leaving Skidegate almost empty for much of each year.

Two things came back to the village with the returning families: wealth, which allowed them to build larger houses and raise more poles, and a variety of diseases that ravaged the populace. Only the influx of survivors from the southern Haida villages that had been hit even harder by disease kept Skidegate alive. The new villagers brought with them many family treasures, which they mostly sold to travellers and collectors.

The worst epidemics hit Skidegate in the late 1860s, and many of the houses abandoned in the back row were never rebuilt, though the frontal poles of these dwellings and their massive frames can be seen in photographs taken by George M. Dawson in 1878.

Two visitors to Skidegate within a short time of each other provide an insight into Haida ceremonial life as the final curtain fell. Reverend William H. Collison of Masset, who visited Skidegate in 1876 with Albert Edward Edenshaw and his son Cowhoe (later baptized George), describes his reception thus (in Lillard 1981:123):

Cedar bark mats were spread for us to the rear of the lodge in the centre . . . Water, soap, and towels were first brought, and each of us invited to wash our hands. The first food offered us was dried salmon and eulachon grease . . . The next dish was boiling dulse, which, when gathered, is made up into square cakes about twelve inches by twelve [30.5 × 30.5 cm] and about one and a half inches [3.8 cm] in thickness, and dried in the sun. Before boiling, this is chopped fine, and it is also mixed with eulachon grease before being served out. Large horn spoons were then handed round, those given to the chiefs being inlaid with abalone or mother-of-pearl. As a special mark of honor, I was given a large silver-plated tablespoon, which became so heated with the boiling seaweed that I could not permit it to touch my lips. Accordingly I called upon them to change it for one of their horn spoons. This caused much hilarity among them to find that the *Yetz haada* preferred a spoon of their manufacture to that made by his own countrymen.

After this dish we were served with dried halibut and grease, and then with boiled herring spawn. During this repast I had remarked two young men, stripped to the waist, beating up in tubs dried berries with water until it became a frothy substance, not unlike ice cream in appearance. This was served up last as dessert.

Dawson attended a potlatch at Skidegate on 24 July 1878 and furnishes a rich description of the proceedings (in Cole and Lockner 1989:478–81):

The smoke from the fire,—which the only light—escaped by wide openings in the roof . . . The performers in this instance about twenty in number, dressed according to no uniform plan but got up in their best clothes, or at least their most gaudy ones, with the addition of certain ornaments &c. appropriate to the occasion. All or nearly all wore head-dresses, variously constructed of cedar bark rope ornamented with feathers &c. or as in one case with a bristling circle of the whiskers of the Sea-lion. Shoulder girdles made of Cedar-bark rope, variously ornamented & coloured, with tassels &c. very common. One man wore gaiters covered with fringes of strung puffin bills which rattled as he moved. Nearly if not all held sprigs of fresh spruce, & were covered about the head with downy feathers which also filled the warm atmosphere of the house. Rattles were also in order. Different from the rest however, five women who stood in front, dressed with some uniformity, Several having the peculiarly beautiful mountain goat shawls which are purchased from the Mainland Indians. The head-dresses of these women were also pretty nearly the same consisting of Small mask faces Carved in wood & inlaid with haliotis [abalone] shell, these Attached to Cedar bark & built round with gay feathers &c. stood above the forehead. The faces of the women—as if All engaged in the dance—gaily painted, vermillion being the favourite colour. Another important feature the master of the ceremonies, who stood in the middle of the back row, slightly higher than the rest, not particularly gaily dressed, but holding a long thin stick with which he kept time & led off the singing . . .

The performer on the drum—a flat tambourine-looking article formed of hide stretched on a hoop—Sat opposite the dancers & near the fire, So that they Could mutually see each others movements. The drum beaten very regularly in "double knocks," thus—tum tum—tum tum—tum tum—&c!

With this the dancers kept time in a sort of Chant or Song to which words appeared Set, & which rose to a loud pitch or fell lower according to the motions of the Master of the Ceremonies, who besides keeping up the time now & then slips in a few words of direction or exhortation. To the drumming the dancing also keeps time, following it closely . . . When the chorus swells to *forte,* the rattles are plied with tenfold vigour & the noise becomes very great. After a performance of ten Minutes or so the Master of Ceremonies gives a sign & all stop, ending with a loud *Hugh!* After a few minutes repose the movement begins again, with the drum.

The people of Skidegate asked Reverend William Duncan of Metlakatla to send a missionary to them, and he sent Edward Mathers, a Tsimshian teacher. This was not what the Haida wanted, so they sent a party led by Chief Nanjingwas to Metlakatla to plead their case again with Reverend Duncan (Lillard 1981:123): "You have gone to Masset . . . and made your residence there, while you have only sent a Tsimshian to teach us. This is not as it should be, as Skidegate was formerly just as powerful as the north, and we should have a white teacher also." This statement illustrates the long-standing rivalry between Skidegate and Masset, and between the Haida and the Tsimshian peoples. That rivalry was one of the driving forces in the production of impressive artworks that are now considered of world significance.

The Methodist mission at Fort Simpson sent the Haida a white teacher, George Robinson, in 1883. The effects of a permanent mission at Skidegate were rapid and profound. Within a year, the traditional plank houses were replaced with single-family dwellings of frame construction, and the rows of houses along the shore were replaced with streets on a grid pattern. The church became the major focus of community life, though there is no evidence that totem poles were destroyed at the instigation of missionaries, as had happened at Masset (Henderson 1974:104).

Edward Dossetter, a Victoria photographer aboard the ship *Rocket,* had stopped at Skidegate in 1881 and took some excellent photographs (PLATE 121). At the time of his visit, several new houses were under construction and a few new memorial poles had been raised, but this activity marked the end of the erection of traditional monuments in the village; the few remaining master carvers received no new commissions after the mid-1880s (PLATE 122).

In 1884, when Richard Maynard, another Victoria photographer who accompanied Newton H. Chittenden on a provincial survey of the Queen Charlotte Islands, visited Skidegate, most of the old houses had been pulled down or were in ruins and many poles had fallen (PLATE 123). The people of Skidegate had decided to adopt the ways of the white man (PLATE 124).

PLATE 121

Chief Nanjingwas wearing a naval uniform (*left*) and another man, probably Chief Skidegate VII, stand before the former's Raven crest at Chief's House in Skidegate. *Photograph by Edward Dossetter, 1881.*

Kiusta

The name Kiusta means "where the trail comes out," in reference to a trail from Lepas Bay to the village. The first European to see the village was Captain George Dixon in July 1787. Kiusta was first portrayed in 1799, in a drawing in the journal of the ship *Eliza,* a fairly accurate panorama of the town from the water. The largest house belonged to the town chief Itl-tini, of a branch of the Stastas Eagles whose head chief was Cunnyha (now Gunia). Cunnyha's house was on Lucy Island near Kiusta, but in about 1800 he moved his people to the Prince of Wales Island area of Alaska to join the group known as the Kaigani Haida.

Kiusta, along with the adjacent village of Yaku, was identified by John Work (in Dawson 1880:173B) as Lu-lan-na. The remains of twelve houses at Kiusta indicate the population was then just over three hundred people.

The name Edenshaw is first mentioned by fur traders of the 1790s. As with all Haida chiefly names, it was passed down the matrilineal line to a chief's eldest sister's son. At least one Chief Edenshaw preceded the one who dominated most of the nineteenth century, Albert Edward Edenshaw. He was born in 1812 and grew up in his uncle's village of Hiellan, but moved to Kiusta after 1834 when he was involved in an unsuccessful attempt to loot the *Vancouver,* a stranded Hudson's Bay Company ship. The captain and crew burned the vessel, nearly killing Edenshaw, but he later salvaged many rifles from the sandbar and replaced their badly burned stocks with ones he carved himself. These he traded to other Haida and converted his new wealth into slaves, of which he eventually owned a dozen.

Albert Edward Edenshaw built his house in Kiusta around 1840 after the details of the carvings on the corner posts, rafter ends and frontal pole were revealed to him in a dream. He named it Story House, and it stood on the site of his predecessor's dwelling, called Property House. When Story House was finished, Albert Edward gave a great potlatch and invited guests from Masset, Skidegate, Kaisun and Cha'atl, as well as from Kaigani Haida villages.

The noted artist Charles Edenshaw, who was Albert Edward's nephew and heir, made a model of Story House for John R. Swanton, and it is now at the American Museum of Natural History in New York (MacDonald 1983:plate 257). Swanton (1905:125–26) notes that Albert Edward intended to leave Story House to his son rather than his nephew, but abandoned the idea and, in fact, the village itself, moving to Kung village in 1850, just before the capture of the ship *Susan Sturgis* by Chief Wiah of Masset.

Just west of Kiusta are three mortuary posts that once supported a communal mortuary box, now completely overgrown with mosses and ferns (PLATE 125). In 1932, Robert Bruce Inverarity (1932:MS 19) saw these mortuary poles and recorded his observations of them:

> The centre pole of the three carved poles was half round, and hollow, while the other two were solid. The two outer poles and the plain pole behind are notched in the top to receive a burial box at a height of about fifteen feet. The box was gone. On both sides of this mortuary

PLATE 124

A number of young Skidegate women wearing secret society regalia are surrounded by men, including Chief Tom Price (*right*) in a white shirt. Reverend Charles Harrison arranged this photograph in 1890 in an attempt to discourage face painting, masks and secret societies. *Photograph by Reverend Charles Harrison.* CMC 71-6778

group were the remains of burial platforms. Both were broken and well pilfered like the cave we had visited, by fisher folk. From the box sides I found there must have been from twenty to thirty boxes on each side of the two platforms.

Remains of the timbers that formed the burial platforms were still evident in the 1990s. The central pole of this mortuary appears to once have been an interior pole of a chief's house, for the back of it is hollowed out, as Inverarity notes above, and it also has a small oval doorway only 30 cm (1 foot) high in the base. The opening is clearly symbolic rather than functional, but it is similar to other known examples of interior central poles from the backs of houses; they appear to be thought of as small frontal poles for the chief's compartment.

When Marius Barbeau went to Kiusta for the Canadian Museum of Civilization in 1939, he photographed several monuments there and at Yaku (PLATE 126). On my first visit to Kiusta in 1967 to map the village, there was but one other pole left standing, with the face of a Bear on it. This carving was removed to the CMC, where a replica was made; the original was then returned to the community museum in Masset (MacDonald 1983:plate 255).

Kung (or Dream Town) was a thriving community of fifteen houses and 280 inhabitants in 1840, according to John Work (in Dawson 1880:173b). On the east side of the village, the remains of a row of houses that appear to be at least several hundred years old suggest an even larger population long ago. The village chief in 1840 was Gulas of the Up-Inlet Town People of the Eagle moiety. A closely related Eagle family shared the eastern half of the town with them, while the Stastas Eagles and a single household of Rose Spit Ravens lived in the western half.

In 1850, Albert Edward Edenshaw, realizing that Kiusta had lost its economic and strategic importance, abandoned his Story House there (Dalzell 1973:443). He resettled at Kung and built an elaborate dwelling named House That Can Hold a Great Crowd of People (PLATES 128, 129). Its architecture has many features of the Kaigani Haida style, such as tall square corner posts, which reveal Chief Edenshaw's strong ties with Haida towns in Alaska. He also erected a pole in the early 1860s in Kung in honour of Governor James Douglas's fairness to native people; the pole portrays Douglas dressed in his frock coat and tall hat. At about the same time, villages in Alaska were raising poles in Abraham Lincoln's honour for freeing the slaves.

About 1875, Albert Edward Edenshaw moved again, this time to Yatze (or Knife Village) at the head of Naden Harbour, in the hope of encouraging more Alaskan trade (PLATES 127, 130). George M. Dawson (1880:163B) notes on his 1878 visit to Kung:

> The village just within the narrow entrance to Virago Sound, from which these people are removing, is called Kung; it has been a substantial and well constructed one, but is now rather decayed, though some of the houses are still inhabited. The houses arranged along the edge of a low bank, facing a fine sandy beach, are eight to ten in number, some of them quite large. The carved posts are not numerous, though in a few instances elaborate.

By the time Newton Chittenden, a provincial government surveyor, stopped at Kung in 1884, it had been abandoned as a permanent village. Yatze had been abandoned the year before, when Albert Edward Edenshaw moved to Masset, but the site continued to be used as a halibut fishing camp until at least the First World War, and smaller temporary houses were built near the beach.

Very few objects were collected at Kung, since it was off the usual visitors' track. Most of the valuable items were taken along by their owners when they moved to Masset. George A. Dorsey, an anthropologist, helped himself to the contents of many Haida graves at Kung, and these objects are now in the Field Museum in Chicago. Dorsey (1897:169) describes one unusual grave (MacDonald 1983:plate 249):

> The grave of the old chief at Kung was the best I had seen. Four short, stout posts had been

This pole was erected by Albert Edward Edenshaw at the village of Yatze in 1878. The bottom figure may have been carved by Charles Edenshaw or John Robson. The Raven at the top sits on a mythic being called Kaga, who was his uncle and with whom he had a quarrel. The Raven landed on Kaga with such force that he split him open. The next figure is a Sea Wolf, followed by a Beaver with prominent incisors. The small figure below that at the front of the pole is a Mountain Hawk, and at the base is a Mountain Goat that is similar to the one on Chief Skedans's mortuary post at Skidegate. *Photograph by Marius Barbeau, 1947.*

House That Can Hold a Great Crowd of People (*left*) was built in the village of Kung by Albert Edward Edenshaw in the 1850s when he moved there from Kiusta. The house next to it (*right*) is Steel House, so called because it was fortified with the addition of extra horizontal planks to the walls so that no one could shoot the inhabitants through the cracks. *Photograph by George M. Dawson, 1878. National Archives of Canada* 264

The interior pole of Albert Edward Edenshaw's house at Kung. The figure at the top is Skungo, a man who dwelt in cave near Kiusta and who was transformed into a monster because he was living on raw fish and birds. The Bear and Frog at the centre are crests often used by Edenshaw, while the large figure at the base looks like a bear but is similar to a being on an interior house pole from Skidegate carved by his nephew Charles Edenshaw (MacDonald 1983:plate 52), which retains its beak and is clearly a Thunderbird.

Photograph by Charles F. Newcombe, 1913.

firmly planted in the ground, and on the inner corners of each grooves had been cut out to receive the beams that supported the little house, in which lay the chief in state. The structure was nearly buried in a thick growth of vegetation, and much work with the axe was needed before the beautifully carved posts could be rendered visible to the camera.

Dorsey (1897:169) explored numerous other graves at Kung, including those of shaman:

What proved of special interest were several very old graves which faced the beach on the east side of the village. These were the burial places of medicine men or Shamans, and quite different from the ordinary grave, instead of a single pole in which the body is placed through a hole in the top or at the side, or from the double pole platform grave which we saw at Kung. We found a little house built of short cedar logs. Inside was placed the Shaman in a long coffin-box reclining at full length with his rattles and other ceremonial paraphernalia about him. With one had been placed several very fine masks, but they were almost entirely crumbled into dust.

PLATE 130

Albert Edward Edenshaw and Wiah, the town chief of Masset, on the beach at Yatze village. *Photograph by George M. Dawson, 1878. National Archives of Canada* 38147

PLATE 131

A panorama of the village of Yan from the south a few years after people began leaving it for Masset. By 1885, Yan was deserted. *Photograph by Edward Dossetter, 1881.*

PLATE 132

Women and children of Yan pose for the camera in front of Flicker House and a memorial pole to an Eagle chief, Ildjiwas. *Photograph by Edward Dossetter, 1881.*

Yan

Yan means Beeline Town (literally, "to proceed in a straight line"). It was a large village of seventeen houses established in the late eighteenth century when a split occurred between two Masset families, one of which, the Masset Inlet Rear-Town People, moved across the inlet to Yan. Other Raven and Eagle families joined them there, but were segregated into Eagles in the north end of town and Ravens in the south.

The town chief of Yan, named Stiltla, was an accomplice of Chief Wiah of Masset in the capture of the ship *Susan Sturgis* in 1852. After its seizure, the ship was brought to Yan, then looted and burned a short distance offshore from Stiltla's House Looking at Its Beak. Stiltla built another large house at Masset, on which he displayed a carved eagle from the stern-board of the ship.

Shortly after photographer Edward Dossetter visited Yan in 1881 when the town was booming, Henry Wiah, the new town chief of Masset, invited the population to move there, and Yan was abandoned (PLATES 131, 132).

178

Kayung

Kayung was an important village from at least the late eighteenth century, and it appears prominently on maps of that period. By the early 1880s, it had been abandoned in the consolidation of north coast villages to Masset that was encouraged by town chief Henry Wiah.

PLATE 133

The remains of Goose House at Kayung village. The frontal pole, which illustrates the myth of the lazy son-in-law, is now in the British Museum. *Photograph by Richard Maynard, 1884.*

One fine pole stood in front of Chief Na'qadjut's House That Wears a Tall Dance Hat, so named in reference to the figure at the top of the pole, a chief wearing a hat with eight rings. The chief's tongue is joined to the tongue of a bearlike animal that he is holding. The depiction of joined tongues is rare on a totem pole, though it was a common feature on argillite carvings in the middle of the last century when this pole was probably created. The middle figure is a Whale with human arms holding its fins. The lowest figure is a Bear with a small Raven in its mouth. This pole was removed from Kayung at the turn of the century by Charles F. Newcombe for E. E. Ayers, a Chicago philanthropist who gave it to the Field Museum. After passing through the hands of several owners, the pole was purchased by the Canadian Museum of Civilization, which painstakingly restored it and erected it in front of the Haida house in the Grand Hall.

A second exquisite pole tells the story of the lazy son-in-law (PLATE 133). The son-in-law is depicted at the level of the gable board on the pole, on the back of a Sea Wolf that is eating a Killer Whale. His mother-in-law, who thinks she has a shaman's power to bring in whales (which in actuality her son-in-law has caught), is lodged above him between two Whales. The house chief holding his club sits at the top.

When Richard Maynard arrived in 1884 to take the first photographs of Kayung, fourteen houses of the old style were still standing. The first five houses at the south end of the village belonged to the Eagles while the remainder all belonged to the Ravens.

Masset

The Haida called this town Uttewas (or White Slope Town), after the shells from countless mollusc dinners of the past scattered on a nearby hill (PLATE 134). The hill itself was called Idjao, and the houses south of it formed a separate village when the first Europeans and New Englanders arrived. The two settlements amalgamated in the middle of the last century to form Masset.

In 1792, while on board the ship *Columbia* commanded by Captain Robert Gray, Joseph Ingraham made a drawing of three villages on Masset Inlet (Holm 1982:233). Probably the one closest to the spit on the east side of the inlet is Masset, the one to the south on the same shore is Kayung and the third village on the western shore is Yan.

The hill at Masset was being used as a fort when Lieutenant Camille de Roquefeuil of France explored the inlet in September 1817 (1823:87–88):

There is something picturesque in the whole appearance of this large village. It is particularly remarkable for the monstrous and colossal figures which decorate the houses of the principal inhabitants, the wide gaping mouths of which serve as a door . . . Ascending the arm of the sea, there is, on the north side, above the largest village, a fort, the parapet of which is covered with beautiful turf, and surrounded by a palisade in good condition.

From the mid-1830s on, the people of Masset and surrounding villages made annual trading voyages to the Hudson's Bay Company post at Fort Simpson on the mainland to sell the quantities of potatoes they grew. Reverend Jonathan Green saw potatoes growing at villages on North Island in 1829 and thought that the Haida had been cultivating them for a long time before his visit (1915:61). In 1839, another visitor to Haida Gwaii, John Dunn, also noted the Haida trade in potatoes (1844:294): "I have known from five to eight hundred bushels traded in one season from these Indians at Fort Simpson." Each spring, large fleets of canoes left Masset to trade at Fort Simpson and to take part in the eulachon fishery at the mouth of the Nass River. The Haida often fought with the Tsimshian on these occasions, as noted in the Hudson's Bay Company journal entry for September 14, 1837.

The first fur trading post on Haida Gwaii was privately established at Masset in 1853, but it was taken over by the Hudson's Bay Company under Alexander McKenzie in 1869. His account of Masset covers nearly a decade and provides many interesting descriptions of Haida activities (McKenzie 1891). The active trade with Europeans and Americans from the late eighteenth century until the arrival of missionaries at Masset in 1873 did little to change Haida beliefs or their symbolic and artistic expressions (PLATE 2). In many ways, they were enriched by new forms of wealth to which they had ready access, and slavery continued here well after it ended elsewhere in Canada and the United States. Around 1850 Chief Albert Edward Edenshaw owned twelve slaves and brought some of them to Masset when he moved there in 1883. George M. Dawson (1880:132B) notes that chiefs in Masset still had slaves at the time of his visit in 1878.

In June 1876, Reverend William H. Collison became the first missionary to take up residence on Haida Gwaii, and his description of arriving at Masset is memorable (in Lillard 1981:86–88):

> We landed in front of the large lodge of the leading chief, Wiah, who was the head of the bear clan at Masset. This numbered among its members the majority of the Masset tribe. The entrance to this lodge was a small oval doorway cut through the base of a large totem, which compelled those entering to bend in order to pass through it. On entering we found ourselves on a tier or gallery of some five or six feet [1.5 or 1.8 m] in width, which formed the uppermost of several similar platforms rising one above the other from the ground floor below, and running all round the house. A stairway led down from this upper platform to the basement or floor. This was the plan on which all the houses were built, the object being defence in case of attack. The small doorway prevented a surprise or rush of an enemy, while

PLATE 134
This view of Masset was taken in 1878 before any European-style houses were built. Within a decade, most of these dwellings had been torn down and the totem poles chopped up for firewood. *Photograph by George M. Dawson. National Archives of Canada* 259

when bullets were flying and crashing through the walls from without, those within remained in safety in the excavated space on the ground floor, in the centre of which was the fireplace.

. . . Around the fire a number of Haida were seated, many of whom, both men and women, had their faces painted in red or black, while some were besmeared with both colours. The chief sat in a peculiarly shaped seat carved out of one piece of wood, a section of a tree, and placed on the first tier or platform, whilst around the fire a number of his slaves were engaged in preparing food.

Chief Wiah welcomed Reverend Collison to his house (PLATES 86, 135, 136, 137) primarily because of the missionary's friendship with Chief Stiltla, Wiah's nearby neighbour, but also because the Haida felt they were losing out to the Tsimshian, who had established a model Christian community under Reverend William Duncan at Metlakatla. Nevertheless, Chief Wiah's greeting was cautious (Collison in Lillard 1981:67–68):

"Your words are good," he replied. "They are wise words. We have heard of the white man's wisdom. We have heard that he possesses the secret of life. He has heard the words of the Chief above. We have seen the change made in the Tsimshian. But why did you not come before? Why did the Iron People not send us the news when it was sent to the Tsimshian? The smallpox which came upon us many years ago killed many of our people. It came first from the north land, from the Iron People who came from the land where the sun sets. Again it came not many years ago, when I was a young man. It came then from the land of the Iron People where the sun rises. Our people are brave in warfare and never turn their backs on their foes, but this foe we could not see and we could not fight. Our medicine men are wise, but they could not drive away the evil spirit, and why? Because it was the sickness of the Iron People. It came from them. You have visited our camps, and you have seen many of the lodges empty. In them the campfires once burned brightly, and around them the hunters and warriors told of their deeds in the past. Now the fires have gone out and the brave men have fallen before the Iron Man's sickness. You have come too late for them!"

He paused, and again his advisers prompted him in low tones, after which he resumed: "And now another enemy has arisen. It is the spirit of the firewater. Our people have learned how to make it, and it has turned friends to foes. This also has come from the land where the sun rises. It is the bad medicine of the *Yetz haada*. It has weakened the hands of our hunters. They cannot shoot as their fathers did. Their eyes are not so clear. Our fathers' eyes were like the eagle's. The firewater has dimmed our sight. It came from your people. If your people had the good news of the Great Chief, the Good Spirit, why did they not send it to us first and not these evil spirits? You have come too late." With these words he sat down.

A few days after arriving in Masset, Collison wrote down an eye-witness account of an important event, a peace ceremony (in Lillard 1981:70):

The following day Edenshaw, an influential chief, arrived from Virago Sound . . . He and his men were received with honours, and a dance of peace was accorded them. There had been a quarrel between the two tribes, and Edenshaw with his leading men had been invited for the purpose of making peace. As their large canoes approached the shore the occupants chanted the brave deeds of the past, and were answered in a similar strain by the concourse of the shore. The chanting was accompanied by regular and graceful motions of the head and body and waving of the hands. The time was kept by a large drum formed like a chest, and made of red cedar wood, painted with grotesque figures, and covered with skin. This was beaten by a drummer seated in the bow of the leading canoe. Naked slaves with their bodies blackened, each bearing a large copper shield, now rushed into the water and cast the shields into the deep, in front of the canoes of the visitors. As these shields are made of native copper, and inscribed with their crests, they are highly valued among the Indians, consequently this was one of the highest marks of welcome and honour. Not that the copper shields were lost to the owners, as they were recovered afterwards on the ebb of the tide.

PLATE 137

The interior of Chief Wiah's Monster House, showing the two deep housepits. There are sleeping compartments on the upper level (*right*). A doorway (*left*) that is covered with pictures from the *London Illustrated News* leads to Wiah's sleeping compartment, which is built outside the house itself. Most of the furniture is from the captured ship *Susan Sturgis. Photograph by Richard Maynard, 1884.*

On landing, the visitors were preceded by a number of dancers, male and female, specially arrayed and with faces painted, who led the way to the lodge prepared for their reception. The central seat was given to Edenshaw, and his leading men were seated around. A messenger now entered to announce the coming of his chief and party to welcome his guests. These at once entered, the chief preceding and followed by the sub-chiefs, and principal men in their dancing attire. The headdress or *shikid* bore the crest of the tribe on the front inlaid with mother-of-pearl, and surmounted by a circlet or crown formed of the bristles of the sea lion, standing closely together so as to form a receptacle. This was filled with swan or eagle's down, very fine and specially prepared. As the procession danced around in front of the guests chanting the song of peace, the chief bowed before each of his visitors. As he did so, a cloud of the swan's-down descended in a shower over his guest. Passing on, this was repeated before each, and thus peace was made and sealed.

The strongest opposition to the missionary came from the shaman, who realized the threat he posed to their traditional practices. Foremost among them was Dr. Kudé (PLATE 138), who was a chief as well as a shaman and who owned a most impressive house in the back row of Masset (MacDonald 1983:plate 202). Dr. Kudé seems to have continued his power struggle with Collison's successor for the Church Missionary Society, for according to Reverend Charles Harrison, who took up his charge in 1882 (in Lillard 1984:168), "he endeavored to persuade the people that the medicine of the Europeans was inevitably fatal to an Indian unless its effect was eradicated by a course of treatment also at his hands." Harrison's description of Kudé (in Lillard 1981:169) agrees with photos of the shaman:

> Kudé, the Masset Shaman, had long tangled hair—it well nigh reached his knees—but when not viably engaged he kept it tied up on top of his head and secured by beautifully carved bone pins. This long hair was believed to assist in his magical power over the evil spirits.

Kudé was finally convinced to cut his hair and become a Christian. He handed over his charms and rattles to Reverend Harrison, who deposited them in the Pitt Rivers Museum at Oxford University.

Albert Edward Edenshaw moved permanently to Masset after old Chief Wiah died in the autumn of 1883. The new chief, Henry Wiah, was neither as wealthy nor as powerful as his predecessor but was well liked by the villagers and welcomed Edenshaw to his town. One of the most significant changes in Masset was the resettlement there of the survivors from all of the other north coast villages after 1883, when Chief Henry Wiah called for old differences to be set aside. People also had a growing desire to live in a community with schools and a mission, as well as a degree of health care (including inoculation against smallpox), which missionaries dispensed along with the gospel.

In 1883, Albert Edward Edenshaw inherited a house at Masset (MacDonald 1983:139, no. 7) from a cousin and, according to Charles F. Newcombe (1898:MS), lived there until his

189

death. A memorial pole that appears to have been erected shortly after he moved into the house has his crests of the Raven and Beaver. The central interior pole also displays his crests, the Raven with frogs in its ears on a Bear, but it may have been installed by his cousin when the house was built; it is now in the Field Museum in Chicago.

Albert Edward Edenshaw appears in almost every traveller's account until his death in 1894. Although he had been suspected of complicity in old Chief Wiah's capture of the *Susan Sturgis* in 1852, Edenshaw's decisive action was acknowledged by the captain with saving his and the crew's lives. Edenshaw successfully negotiated their release in return for a ransom from the Hudson's Bay Company at Fort Simpson, and a marble memorial to this feat was erected in front of Henry Edenshaw's Property House in the middle of Masset. Albert Edward also owned a house at Klinkwan village in Alaska, and his house in Masset had a fine frontal pole and a memorial post topped with a huge figure of a Bear, similar to the figure of a Bear in Kiusta. His nephew Charles Edenshaw, the famous carver, later resided in this house and may have placed the name board "Edenshaw" over the door to advertise his art works for sale to travellers (PLATE 139). In the late 1890s, the dwelling was replaced by the modest frame house where Charles Edenshaw lived until his death in 1924.

Hiellan

Hiellan was a town of some importance in the early nineteenth century, and an impressive fort stood on the opposite side of the mouth of the Hiellan River on Graham Island. Both Haida and Tsimshian myths include accounts of its tricky defences and the battles fought there. Hiellan belonged to two branches of Eagles. The leading Eagle chief, Sqilao, was closely related to the first known Chief Edenshaw who was the uncle of Albert Edward Edenshaw and for whom the triple mortuary at Kiusta was erected.

The only surviving house frontal pole at Hiellan was photographed by Harlan I. Smith of the Canadian Museum of Civilization in 1919 (PLATE 140). It had stood there for over a century before it was transported in 1947 to Prince Rupert, where it was placed by the road into town to welcome visitors. After a short sojourn in Victoria at the Royal British Columbia Museum, the pole was returned to Masset. The shed in which the pole was stored collapsed under the snow load in the winter of 1993, and it was moved into Haida artist Jim Hart's carving shed, where it awaits replication.

This pole and the triple mortuary at Kiusta were both carved around 1820 by Sqiltcange, who came from Tsal village. Both monuments emphasize large Bear figures with a myriad of small figures emerging from their joints and orifices. The poles are unique in providing examples of the archaic style of Haida art similar to that seen by the first Europeans to visit Haida Gwaii.

KAIGANI HAIDA

PLATE 141

The house of Henry
Edenshaw's father-in-law at
Klinkwan rivalled that of
Chief Wiah of Masset in the
elaborately sculptured posts of
its facade. *Photograph from
Alaska-Yukon-Pacific
Expedition, circa 1888–89.* CMC
72-9544

At least fifty years before Europeans first made contact with the Haida, some Haida families had reacted to growing pressures on the population of the villages around North Island by beginning to move to the islands of what is now the Prince of Wales archipelago in southeast Alaska. Another reason for the move may have been to position themselves closer to the Russian trading posts at Wrangell and Sitka that supplied important materials as well as new objects of wealth.

According to traders' accounts of the late eighteenth century, the families of Dadens village on Haida Gwaii were actively relocating to southeast Alaska to the extent that it was virtually abandoned as a permanent village by the early nineteenth century. Slowly, the Haida replaced the Tlingit-speaking people who had occupied the area for thousands of years; however, the original Tlingit place names survive, at least in part, in many Kaigani Haida village names. Eventually, the Haida towns and camps included Kaigani itself, a camp that waned as initial immigrants moved on to other settlements, including the larger more permanent villages of Klinkwan, Sukkwan, Howkan and Kasaan.

Klinkwan

Klinkwan is the Haida version of a Tlingit name meaning Shellfish Town. The village stretched around several bays and contained upwards of twenty houses, though John R. Swanton's informants (1905:294) remembered the names of only thirteen of them. John Work (in Dawson 1880:173B), who compiled a population estimate between 1836 and 1841, identifies it as Clickass in reference to the nearby river and assigns it a total of 417 inhabitants. All the families belonged to the Raven moiety.

One prominent resident of Klinkwan was Albert Edward Edenshaw's son Henry, whose house expressed true opulence in Haida terms. This was the only house interior on the entire Northwest Coast that was a rival to the grand interior of the Whale House of the Tlingit at Klinkwan (Emmons 1916), but unfortunately, not one interior element of Edenshaw's house survives: only a photograph bears witness to its grandeur (PLATE 142). In the adjacent house, which belonged to Henry's father-in-law, all three exterior poles display the Dragonfly crest: the central pole was by far the tallest in the village, and both front corner posts are elaborately carved. The large central pole has a Beaver at its base, with a small Beaver between its paws and frogs emerging from its ears. Above them, a Bear holds an insect in its mouth. Next is a *tcamaos* (a supernatural snag that devoured canoes), a Crane with a long beak, and nine potlatch rings. The Raven sits on top.

The left corner post portrays the Bear Mother story, originally a Tsimshian myth in which a berry picker slips on the dung of a grizzly bear and curses her luck. She is abducted by bears and becomes the wife of the Chief of the Bears; their two offspring can appear as human children or bear cubs. She and her children are eventually rescued by her brothers,

PLATE 142 (facing page)

The interior of Henry Edenshaw's house at Klinkwan village, Alaska. The interior pole has a Thunderbird (missing its

beak). Henry Edenshaw's father, Albert Edward Edenshaw, probably carved and decorated the house. On the walls of

the housepit, carved and painted storage box fronts alternate with images of coppers, providing a lavish appearance.

Photograph by Charles F. Newcombe. CMC 71-4705

PLATE 143

In 1901, a potlatch was staged in order to mark the move from Klinkwan village to Hydaburg, Alaska, as well as the

abandonment of ceremonial regalia. Participants include (*left to right*): Robert Edenshaw (with drum), Matthew

Collison (kneeling as Grizzly Bear-of-the-Sea), an unknown man wearing a Chilkat blanket, Eddie Scott, Eddie Cojo,

Donald Mikatla, Antkleg (Mike George), Ben Duncan and Nasank (Adam Spoon's son). *Photograph by Winter and

Pond, 1901.* CMC J2822

who kill her husband. At the base of the pole is a Bear eating a man, another Bear with an insect in its mouth, and a Hawk.

The right corner post has at its base a Bear holding an insect (a reference to the Bear Mother story), another Bear holding the berry picker from the Bear Mother story between its paws, and a human holding the baby Raven in a moon. The portrayal of the berry picker's long hair and breasts are unusually naturalistic for Haida art.

In Henry Edenshaw's house, the interior post depicts an insect between the arms of a Bear with humanlike hands. These figures sit between the ears of the Thunderbird, whose once prominent beak has fallen off, leaving only a mortise joint. A small arched doorway through the breast of the Thunderbird is symbolic only and leads to a compartment at the back of the house. The planks that formed the wall of this compartment are missing but were undoubtedly highly decorated.

The housepit walls were also elaborately carved and painted (PLATE 142). In fact, there were two sets of walls, each supporting two steps down to the firepit. The walls of the terraces were composed of huge hewn planks some 10 cm (4 inches) thick and about a metre (3 feet) wide. The top row consisted of carved and painted chests alternating with elaborately decorated copper shields; there were six coppers and five storage boxes on each side, for a total of twenty-four coppers and twenty carved and painted boxes. The lower terrace was bounded by two coppers (in a diagonal position) and three chests, for a total of eight coppers and twelve chests. In all, sixty-four symbols of great wealth surrounded the house pit.

The last potlatch held in Klinkwan in 1901, before the Haida left the village and moved to Hydaburg, was the subject of a famous photograph (PLATE 143). All the participants are costumed in their treasures, including Chilkat blankets, painted leather capes, bearskin robes and trade blankets adorned with crests outlined in dentalium shells. They wear frontlets and peaked shaman's hats as well as carved wooden crest helmets (PLATE 144). Masks, cedar bark neckrings of the secret societies, Raven rattles and drums complete the tableau immortalized forever in silver nitrate. This potlatch marked a shift in the cultural paradigm, as proud lineage heads, each with their own links to the supernatural, became colonized wage earners and sold their treasures (PLATE 145). Ronald Weber (1985), an anthropologist at the Field Museum in Chicago (which now possesses much of this regalia), has identified most of the people and items in the photograph.

The house that formed the backdrop of this potlatch was called House Standing Up. The building belonged to the town chief whose name meant "one unable to buy," since he once had owned a copper that a rival chief was unable to afford. It was a suitable setting for the final ceremony.

PLATE 144

On this Sculpin crest helmet, the nine finely woven rings mark the number of feasts that the owner has hosted.
Collected at Klinkwan village in Alaska before 1901 by George T. Emmons for the Lord Bossom collection. CMC VII-B-1437 (S92-4303)

197

Sukkwan

Sukkwan is the Haida version of a Tlingit name meaning Town on the Fine Underwater Grass, a reference to the edible seaweed that grows there. John Work (in Dawson 1880:173B) claimed it had a population of 229 people in the period between 1836 and 1841, including both Ravens and Eagles. Sukkwan was situated on a point of land, with five houses on the south side of the point and seven on the north. John R. Swanton (1905:294) recorded the names of seven houses, including Grizzly Bear House, Cedarbark Skin House, and Clay House (because it was painted with clay). Another was called Watery House after the name of a house at Kiusta, the town from which the people of Sukkwan came.

The pole of the middle house on the north side has a most unusual figure of the lazy son-in-law holding a small Whale in each hand (PLATE 146). He wears a tall chief's hat with three potlatch rings, around which a strange creature is wrapped. It may be a Bullhead, judging by its prominent ribs at the back and its pointed horns, which are firmly grasped by the watchman figure on the top. The son-in-law stands on a Wasgo (or Sea Wolf), which has the small figure of a chief crouched between its ears; inside the ears are curved hornlike devices. The Wasgo also holds an insect in its mouth and has a small human between its knees. Sukkwan was abandoned in the late 1890s, and this pole was taken to the totem park at Hydaburg during a reclamation project in the 1930s.

Howkan

Howkan is first mentioned by John Work (in Dawson 1880:173B) as being a sizable town of 458 inhabitants. The name is a Tlingit one. Ensign Albert P. Niblack (1890:386), who explored the coast of Alaska for the U.S. Navy, claims that the original inhabitants of the camp called Kaigani moved their winter residence to Howkan. Some remained at the small village of Koianglas just below Howkan but were in the process of amalgamating with Howkan when he observed them. Niblack (1890:385) claims that in 1886 Howkan was thriving and had a winter population of about three hundred.

During the last twenty years of the previous century, photographs recorded rapid changes in the houses and poles throughout the village. Perhaps the most radical change, but one that took place in stages, can be seen in Chief Skowl's house. He was town chief of both Howkan and Kasaan. His house in Howkan sat near the centre of town. After he died in the winter of 1882–83, his successor lost no time in adding a second storey to the house by putting joists through the roof and building a European-style cottage on top, complete with a balcony and gingerbread trim. He also added milled lumber and five windows to the facade of the old house.

The pole in front of Chief Skowl's house has a naturalistic American eagle on the top, flanked by two traditional watchmen. Below that is a figure of the Czar of Russia with flowing locks and a beard. He wears a coat with epaulets and stands between the ears of the

PLATE 145

This memorial pole from Howkan village in Alaska tells the myth of Qingi and the flood. When the Great Flood came, all of the villagers had to climb up on the chief's hat to avoid drowning. This pole was displayed at the Century of Progress World's Fair in London, England, in 1951. It is shown here in the rotunda of the old Canadian Museum of Civilization in Ottawa. *Acquired before 1901 by George T. Emmons for the Lord Bossom collection.* CMC VII-B-1557 (s80-254)

PLATE 146

The frontal pole *(left)* of this house at Sukkwan portrays the lazy son-in-law holding two Whales and standing on a Wasgo (Sea Wolf). The figure at the top on which the human figure rides is either a Bullhead or a *tcamaos* (supernatural snag). In the centre, a very old mortuary provides the Raven with a spruce sapling for a headdress. *Photograph by W. T. Lopp, circa 1890.* CMC 99400

PLATE 147

This memorial pole *(centre)* from Howkan village in Alaska is arguably the finest Haida carving ever done. The strong diagonal lines help to interlock the multitude of figures, and the deep carving and rich detailing enhance the overall effect. The central portion of the pole illustrates the myth about the lazy son-in-law. It is tempting to think this was the pole at Howkan that Albert Edward Edenshaw carved after he had a dream about what to put on it. The pole was erected in a public park in Indianapolis and later destroyed. A replica of it was erected in Indianapolis in 1996. *Photograph by Julius Sternberg, 1922.*

Thunderbird that sports an incredible display of plumage on its head, wings, breast, tail and even its feet. At the base, a standing Bear holds an insect in its mouth.

Another remarkable pole was erected next door to Chief Skowl's house in about 1885. A photo of the pole, taken much later, depicts its intricately detailed interlocking figures (PLATE 147).

The graveyard at Howkan is perhaps the most elaborate of any Haida village and included full-sized totem poles that were erected as memorials to the deceased, as well as a large figure of a Killer Whale with a very tall dorsal fin, a full-scale replica of which flanks the entrance to the Burke Museum in Seattle. At Howkan, George T. Emmons acquired a memorial pole, two Sea Lion house posts (PLATE 85) and the remarkable interior house screen (PLATE 149) that once stood between them for the collection of Lord Bossom in London; they were repatriated to the Canadian Museum of Civilization in the 1960s after Lord Bossom's death.

Kasaan

Kasaan is originally a Tlingit word meaning Beautiful Town. The town chief, named Skowl, had a large house situated towards the north end of the settlement. When George T. Emmons first visited the village in 1885, he took a photo of old Chief Skowl's house after it had been freshly clad with milled siding (PLATE 150). Chief Skowl also owned a second house in the village that had an unusual frontal pole (PLATE 151).

Albert P. Niblack witnessed the funeral ceremonies for old Chief Skowl (PLATE 152), who died in the winter of 1882–83 (1890:plate LXVII caption):

> According to the custom of the region, his body was first displayed in state dressed in the ceremonial robes of a chief. Later it was enclosed in a casket and deposited, as shown, on a pile of boxes containing his clothing and ceremonial dance paraphernalia.

The second house belonging to Chief Skowl was also an impressive building; it was the last one at the north end of the second row. The frontal pole incorporates more non-Haida motifs and styles than any other piece; in fact, the only traditional element is the Eagle on top. Another Eagle with its head to one side is clearly an American eagle copied from a coin or a ship's figurehead. The figures on the pole include three Russians and one angel. The Russians are priests dressed in large flowing robes, hands crossed on their breasts—or pointing to heaven, as in the figure at the top. The angel, whose face is surrounded on three sides by feather designs, is a particular delight. Other spaces, usually filled on traditional Haida poles by diminutive animal figures emerging from the orifices of larger figures, are decorated here with tendril and leaf patterns copied from the stylized ship carvings common at the time. This pole was transported to Ketchikan, where it was placed in the midst of traffic beside a tunnel.

PLATE 150
Kasaan village in Alaska, with the house of Chief Skowl, who died in 1882–83, at the right. By the time this photograph was taken, his successor had added milled siding and windows to the house. The Raven stealing the sun poles of both the old and new chief flank the stairway that leads up from the beach. *Photograph by George T. Emmons.* CMC 71-4709

PLATE 151

This pole, in front of a second house in Kasaan belonging to Chief Skowl, depicts priests, an angel and Eagles. Rather than celebrating the arrival of the Russian Orthodox Church in Alaska, however, it ridicules the fact that young men from the villages wanted to train for the priesthood and abandon the old ways. *Photograph by A. Bergstresser, circa 1900.* CMC 71-4707

PLATE 152

For nearly two years after his death, the body of Chief Skowl lay in state inside his house at Kasaan, Alaska. The burial chest, draped with a button blanket, is surrounded by storage chests filled with his regalia; beside the burial chest are his eight copper shields. The people in the photo are his slaves, who were displayed as part of his wealth. *Photograph by Albert P. Niblack, 1883*

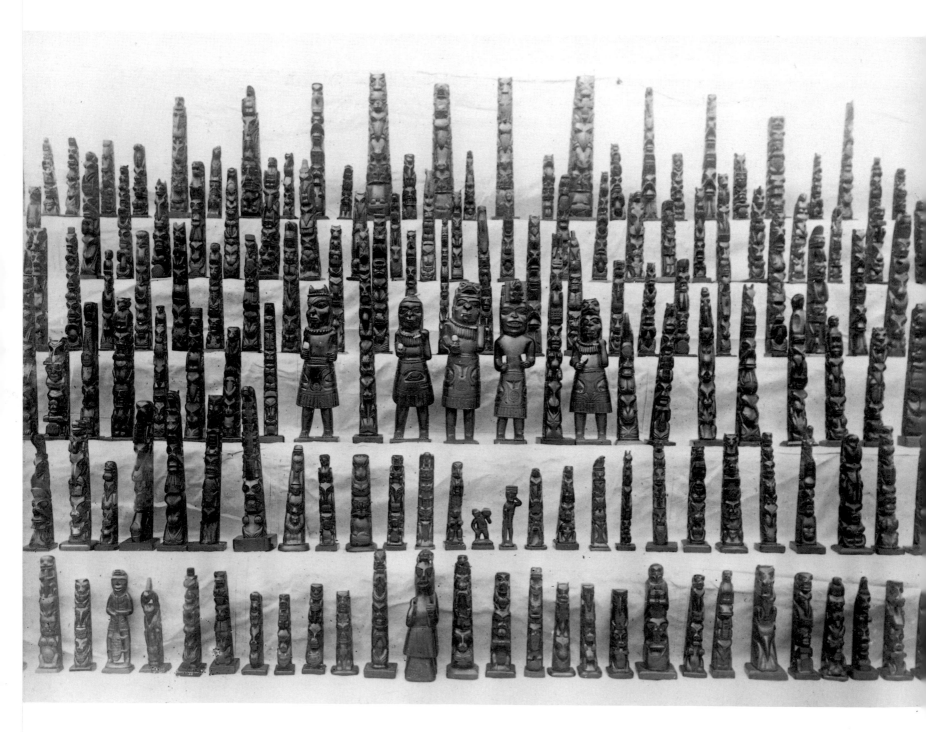

ARTISTS OF THE GOLDEN AGE | Chapter Seven

The golden age of Haida art lasted half a century, beginning in the 1850s when new markets opened in Victoria and elsewhere that stimulated both greater production and the development of new art forms, until the collapse of the Haida population at the beginning of the twentieth century. During this period, large objects were replaced by smaller replicas that could easily be taken home by tourists as mementoes of their visits to the Northwest Coast (PLATES 76, 153). It was a golden age because there was not only a great number of Haida artists who were well trained in their traditional style yet felt free to innovate and create new expressions of their rich heritage but also because there was a large and eager market for their work.

Many Haida artists successfully made the transition to creating pieces for another cultural milieu where having an identifiable style was essential in the marketplace. Even so, signing their work was not an accepted practice, and many artists resisted it, preferring to express themselves through subtle variations on traditional style (Wright 1985). This has resulted in endless speculation among scholars who pen articles with titles like "Will the Real Charles Edenshaw Please Stand Up?" (Holm 1981:75). At least one thesis (Davidson 1967) and several articles have been written on Charles Edenshaw, of which the best are by Bill Holm (1981) and Alan Hoover (1983, 1995). The work of carver Tom Price (PLATES 103, 154) also has been the subject of study (Gessler 1971:245–52 and Holm 1981:193–97). Bill Holm (1981:176–77) originally defined one body of work as that of the Masset artist Gwaitilth, but later found evidence that it was by another Masset artist named Simeon Stiltla (RAIN 1980). Marius Barbeau (1953, 1957) published short studies of many Masset and Skidegate artists of a later period.

ALBERT EDWARD EDENSHAW

Albert Edward Edenshaw was a living link between the traditional world of the Haida, uninterrupted for centuries, and the chaotic world of the historical era (PLATE 155). His achievements as a chief are recorded in the histories of many north coast villages including Kiusta, Dadens, Kung, Yatze, Hiellan and Masset. He has taken on legendary significance, partly because of the numerous if brief references to him in the logs and journals of ships' captains, traders and missionaries throughout much of the nineteenth century. His undisputed contribution was in laying the groundwork for his successors to nurture the fundamentals of Haida culture and assure its survival.

PLATE 153

The personal collection of model argillite pole carvings amassed by Thomas Deasey, the Indian agent at Masset early in this century. The artists represented include Charles Edenshaw. The collection is now at the Florida State Museum, Gainesville. *Photograph by Harlan I. Smith, 1919.* CMC 46701

PLATE 154

An oval argillite platter with a very compact design of a Wasgo, or Sea Wolf. It has both legs and fins, and a long wolflike tail curves over its back. The inverted crescent-shaped slits in the eye forms and other details identify it as the work of the Skidegate carver Tom Price (Chief Ninstints). *Acquired before 1899 for the A. Aaronson collection.* CMC VII-B-760 (s82-265)

PLATE 155

Chief Albert Edward Edenshaw dressed in naval uniform at about eighty years of age. After a long career of warfare, slave trading, art, gold prospecting and possible piracy, he appointed his nephew Charles Edenshaw as his successor and settled down to be a strong supporter of the Methodist Church. His life spanned the era in which the Haida went from being feared as the Vikings of the Pacific to near extinction. *Photograph by Robert Reford, circa 1890. National Archives of Canada* c60824

Albert Edward Edenshaw, who was born in 1812 south of Rose Spit, inherited the title of Chief Edenshaw about 1832 upon the death of his uncle, the first Chief Edenshaw of Dadens. By this time, Dadens had been abandoned as a permanent village. He moved to Kiusta and built Story House, the decorations for which had come to him in a dream (Swanton 1905:125–26, plate IV). It is then that he probably honed his own skills as a canoe maker and especially as a craftsman in copper and steel (PLATE 156). One of his specialties was elaborately decorated steel war daggers.

In 1853, Albert Edward moved to Kung, where he built House That Can Hold a Great Crowd of People (PLATE 128). At the top of the house's frontal pole is a Bear holding two figures: one is a human riding on the back of a Dragonfly. This may represent the vision that he had received in the 1830s when he married a Kaigani Haida woman from Klinkwan, and the town chief asked him to carve a totem pole, an event that launched his career in woodcarving. Alfred Adams, a Masset chief, describes the effect of this early commission (in Barbeau, no date:file 253.3):

> He got inspiration drinking medicine and he would fast and get his imagination and his con-
> ception of different stories and legends. His [son] (Henry) told me that his father never was a
> carver when young, not a public carver. But once he was visiting in Howkan (Prince of Wales
> Island) and was hired to make a carving there of a big totem pole . . . When he got to the big
> tree he visualized then what he was to put on. That is how he started but he had not done
> very much of this before.

Edenshaw and his clansmen regularly participated in the sea otter and fur seal hunt that yearly took them back to Dadens. The single pole that stood there was carved by Edenshaw and raised in the late nineteenth century next to the house he built there for his second wife, Amy (MacDonald 1983:plate 263). At the top is a Bear on a stack of seven potlatch cylinders, and below that is the Raven from the story about the halibut fisherman. The next figure is characteristic of his work; it represents the berry picker that the Haida see in the dark pattern of the moon and relates to a myth associated with his wife Amy's lineage. The small Frog hanging below the moon disk is another favourite of the artist and appears on his poles at Kung and elsewhere. Towards the base is a Grizzly Bear with two cubs, one in its mouth and the other between its legs. Another small human figure is crouched between the Bear's knees and stands on the lowest figure, probably a Whale.

The two human figures are exceptionally well carved, more graceful and animated than most Haida depictions of humans. The figure of a woman with long hair on the right-hand post of the house at Klinkwan (PLATE 141) that belonged to Henry's father-in-law, is a strong indication that Albert Edward carved the whole sculptured facade. The elaborate interior carvings inside Henry's house may also be his work (PLATE 142), since his characteristic Drag-onfly is on the left corner post. The house was probably built in the 1870s.

Some time after 1883, Albert Edward moved to Masset. A pair of memorial poles at the

PLATE 156

This very large copper shield, 117 cm (46 inches) high, once belonged to Albert Edward Edenshaw. He was a talented shield engraver and sold his decorated coppers as far south as the Fraser River. This copper portrays his female Grizzly Bear crest. *Purchased from Mary Yaltatse of Masset in 1970.* CMC VII-B-1595 (S92-4312)

northern corner of his house there displayed three important crests. The first pole had a Beaver at the top and the Raven below. The second memorial pole had a standing Frog with potlatch cylinders at the top and a standing Beaver at the base (MacDonald 1983:plate 178). It is not known whether or not these two poles were carved by either Albert Edward or Charles Edenshaw, or by both.

According to tradition, Albert Edward chose Charles Edenshaw, the son of his sister Qwa'Kuna, to be his successor. When Albert Edward passed away in 1894, Charles not only took over the mantle of Chief Edenshaw but raised the artistic heritage of his famous uncle to new heights.

JOHN ROBSON

Little is known about John Robson until the late 1860s when he succeeded his uncle as Chief Giatlins, a Raven lineage chief in Skidegate (PLATE 103); at the same time he inherited Grizzly Bear's Mouth House, one of the most splendid buildings in the village (PLATE 122). Robson was a noted carver of totem poles from the late 1860s until the custom of raising large poles fell into disfavour around 1885. He also produced many house models and works in argillite (PLATES 83, 157).

Robson married Qwa'Kuna, the widowed mother of Charles Edenshaw. Robson taught his stepson many carving skills and worked on a number of poles with him, which explains the points of similarity in their styles.

One fine example of the artistic collaboration between Charles Edenshaw and John Robson is an elaborately carved memorial pole in front of House Upon Which Storm Clouds Make a Noise in Skidegate. The top figure of a Whale is similar to the one on Chief Skidegate's interior pole. John Robson later made a model of it for John R. Swanton (1905:plate VIII-4). The two carvers may also have worked together on a large mortuary post raised in 1879–80 by Chief Skidegate and his wife in honour of Chief Skedans.

216

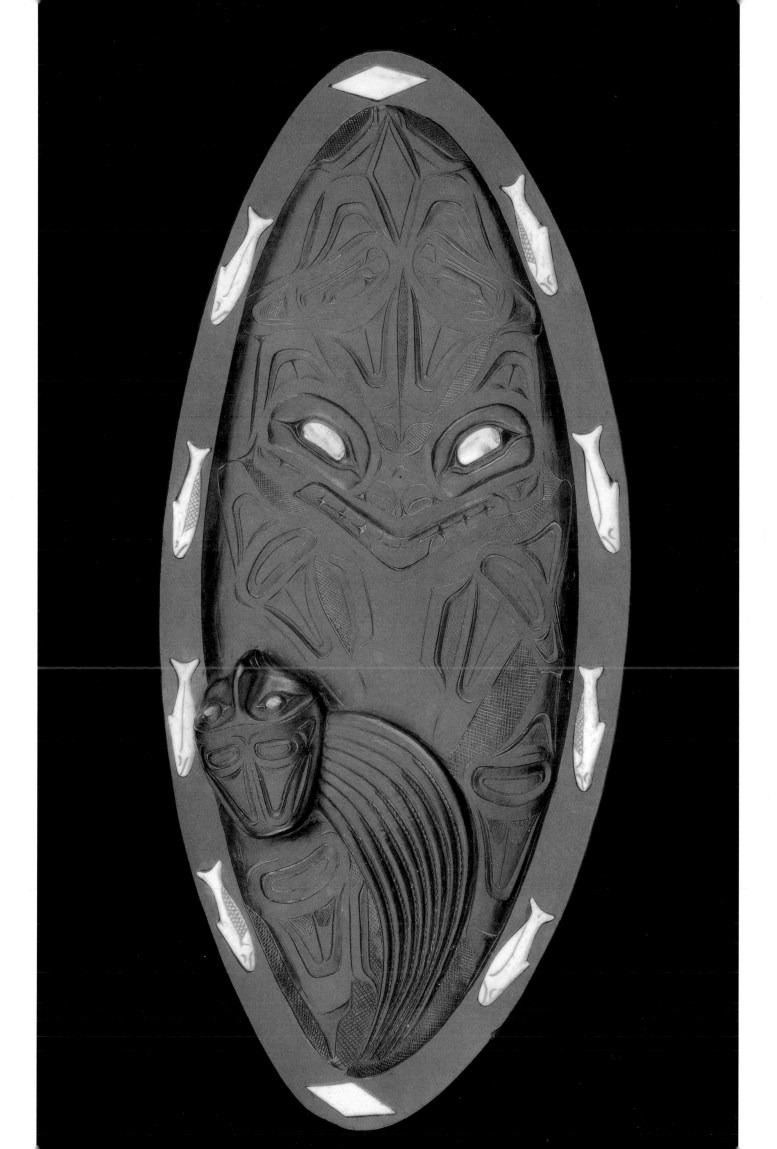

Charles Edenshaw, or Tahayren, was born in 1839 to Albert Edward Edenshaw's only sister, Qwa'Kuna. According to Charles's daughter Florence Edenshaw Davidson (in Blackman 1982:72), her father started carving argillite when he was fourteen and had to stay in bed sick.

Between 1878 and 1881, John Robson raised a memorial pole to Qwa'Kuna, carved by Charles, with the Raven, Beaver and Eagle perched on top (MacDonald 1983:plates 36, 39). The Raven on it is similar to the one on which the figure of Governor James Douglas stands on Albert Edward Edenshaw's "friendship" pole at Kung. Charles may have been an apprentice carver to his uncle on the Kung pole. In his mid-teens, Charles joined his uncle at Kung every summer, and the time he spent there is evident in the exquisite detail of the house model he created of Albert Edward's Story House. After reaching maturity, Charles moved to Masset to apprentice further with his uncle. According to Alfred Adams (in Barbeau, no date:file 251.14):

> While training in his uncle's workshop, Charles perfected his knowledge of ancient traditions, perfected his technique and learned to observe nature . . . To mark his acquiring the master craftsman's position in the community, he gave a potlatch, or feast for the village, in his uncle's home.

Charles married Isabella K'woiyang, whose Aunt Amy was the second wife of Albert Edward. In the 1870s, he carved two poles for Chief Skidegate. The first was an interior house post of a Whale, a Frog and the Raven with a long beak (MacDonald 1983:plate 46). The second, which he may have worked on with John Robson, was a mortuary pole for one of Chief Skidegate's wives, erected in 1879–80. The human figure on it was said to represent the lazy son-in-law story in which a youth killed a Wasgo (or Sea Wolf) in the lake behind Skidegate (MacDonald 1983:plate 146). The face on the pole is a *tcamaos* (supernatural snag).

Charles's skills and repertoire expanded gradually to include work in wood, argillite and precious metals (PLATES 79, 96, 99, 135, 158). In the 1890s, his artistry and traditional knowledge came to the attention of anthropologists and museum collectors engaged in the frantic effort to record and collect Haida art and culture before it died, including Charles F. Newcombe, Franz Boas and especially John R. Swanton. The Indian agent at Masset, Thomas Deasey, also kept him busy with orders for model argillite poles (PLATE 153).

Charles and Isabella had five daughters but only two sons, both of whom died young. To ease his loss, Charles began teaching many young carvers Haida myths and the techniques of carving in a range of materials. Among those he taught were John Marks, Isaac (Ben) Chapman and Daniel Stanley (Skilgoldzo), the grandson of renowned Masset artist Simeon Stiltla.

PLATE 158
A charming example of an argillite platter by Charles Edenshaw with a classic Thunderbird and Whale design. The double outline of formlines and changes of texture in background areas mark this piece as his, although neither he nor other carvers of that time signed their work. *Acquired at Masset before 1899 for the A. Aaronson collection.* CMC VII-B-824 (S94-6817)

Charles Edenshaw's style is very distinctive, with very bold formlines. For Haida clients, he made pieces for personal adornment or practical use. Silver and gold jewellery, including earrings and finger rings, brooches and bracelets were in demand by both Haida and tourists (PLATE 159). His wife, Isabella, wove baskets and hats that he painted with designs, mostly for sale to tourists (PLATES 16, 17). Argillite carvings for tourists represented most of his output, including inkstands, model houses, lidded chests and large platters (PLATE 158). One of his major works, a traditional Haida burial chest, is in the Canadian Museum of Civilization (PLATE 96).

Charles Edenshaw died in Masset in 1924, leaving his tools to his nephew Charles Gladstone, a carver in Skidegate and the grandfather of noted artist Bill Reid.

The momentum of the golden age of Haida art came to an end as lineage groups broke down into separate family units and Christianization turned Haida myths into the equivalent of fairy tales. Argillite carvings continued to be sold through intermediaries to tourist shops in Victoria and Vancouver, but as tourist values took over the market, argillite poles were priced by the inch, and the pride of individual craftsmanship virtually disappeared.

After the last two artists of the golden age died, Charles Edenshaw in 1924 and John Cross in 1939, Rufus Moody and a number of others did what they could to bridge the gap until a new generation of sophisticated artists, many of them trained in art schools, rekindled the flame that led to the renaissance of Haida art beginning in the 1950s and 1960s.

PLATE 159
Charles Edenshaw carving a silver bracelet amidst examples of his argillite model poles and a box. The damage to his left eye from a revolver accident bothered him as he got older but did not affect the exquisite sense of balance and symmetry in his carving. *Photographer unknown, circa 1880.* CMC 88926

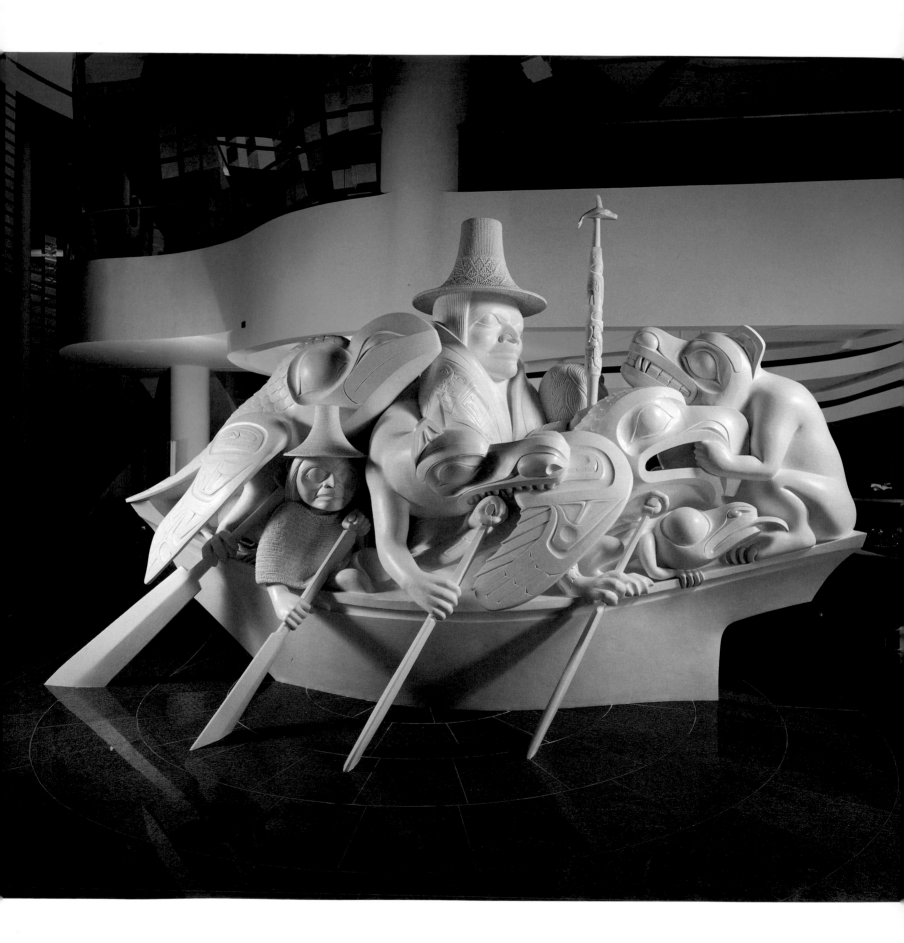

DEATH AND REBIRTH OF THE RAVEN | Chapter Eight

The world is highly sensible of the loss incurred when a species of bird or fish is lost to extinction, yet we are less concerned with the loss of a unique culture. Perhaps, like the survivors of the Black Plague, we celebrate our own survival while ignoring the destruction of others. The age of colonization was just such a plague in the cultural history of humankind. Countless thousands of cultures that had survived and thrived for millennia in various pockets of the earth's habitats suddenly were swamped by warfare and pestilence such as they had never known before. The Haida stand as an example of that physical and cultural decimation.

When the first European sailor spotted the shores of Haida Gwaii in 1774, the Haida population stood at close to twelve thousand, counting both the Prince of Wales archipelago and Haida Gwaii (the Queen Charlotte Islands). By the turn of the century, that population had been dramatically reduced to less than five hundred. Most indigenous peoples in the New World lost 90 per cent of their population to their collision with Europeans. The Haida lost more than 95 per cent.

When I began research on Haida Gwaii in 1966, the number of fluent Haida speakers was estimated at less than forty. Today, programs in the schools have helped those figures to begin to grow, but it still remains to be seen if the Haida can achieve what the Maori of New Zealand have done with their concept of "language nests" (interactive groups) as brooders of indigenous language. The isolation of the Maori from other large populations and their current position as more than 10 per cent of the population of New Zealand provide safer ground for optimism than for the Haida, overwhelmed as they are by English speakers. Even on their own islands they are a minority of the population, although this may change in the next few decades.

The renaissance of Haida culture, however, is attributable to a growing number of artists (PLATE 160). Bill Holm (1990:606–7) notes that the formline style of Northwest Coast art is calligraphic in principle: that is, there is an implicit grammar at play in each work that determines the message of the piece. In a wonderful interplay between anthropologists, art historians and the new generation of Haida artists, this grammar has been revived and extended.

PLATE 160

The original plaster pattern for Bill Reid's bronze sculpture *The Spirit of Haida Gwaii*, now in the Canadian Museum of Civilization. The first bronze cast (called *The Black Canoe*) stands before the Canadian Embassy in Washington, D.C., and the second one (called *The Jade Canoe*) is the centrepiece of the Vancouver airport. CMC (s92-9152)

The renaissance of Haida art begins with a story that has become apocryphal. One fateful day in 1956, Bill Reid, whose mother was a Haida from Skidegate and whose father was a German American, was reading the news as an announcer for CBC Radio in Vancouver: the news item that changed his life was about a grant to recreate the totem poles and houses of a Haida village on the campus of the University of British Columbia (PLATE 161). Reid says that he turned off his microphone right after the newscast and phoned the university's Museum of Anthropology to offer his assistance in pursuing this goal. It proved to be his apprenticeship in rediscovering Haida art and led to almost a half century of pioneering work in cultural reconstruction.

Bill Reid honed his skills over many years through replicating works created by his fore-bears, especially his great, great uncle, Charles Edenshaw. He studied the several hundred pieces of gold and silver jewellery by Charles Edenshaw in museums and copied images from John R. Swanton's *Contributions to the Ethnography of the Haida,* from Franz Boas's *Primitive Art* and from books by Marius Barbeau on Haida myths and argillite carvings.

This apprenticeship period led to a mature artistry in gold and silver jewellery that set new standards of value among eager collectors and has been well documented (Shadbolt 1986). Eventually, Reid undertook a series of public sculptures, each of which took the art world by surprise because of its increasing innovativeness, not to mention ever-growing scale. These completely new works went far beyond traditional prototypes and brought an indigenous style for the first time to the national level in Canada. Ultimately, Reid's work was recognized on the international level with exhibits in Paris, Budapest, Tokyo and Washington.

Beginning with his large cedar sculpture titled *The Raven and the First Men,* commissioned in 1980 by Dr. Walter Koerner for the Museum of Anthropology at the University of British Columbia, Reid pushed Haida art into a format well beyond the house frontal pole or mortuary post. His second work on a large scale, the bronze *Killer Whale* for the Vancouver Aquarium in 1984, is closely related to Charles Edenshaw's compotes or fruit dishes that featured pivotal figures of Haida cosmology as the handle of the lid (PLATE 163). A prototype for this sculpture was the gold box he made for the Royal British Columbia Museum in 1971, on which the tightly arched Whale forms the handle of the lid. This Whale is all of 7.6 cm (3 inches) high while the monumental bronze version is 5.5 m (18 feet) high. His next large piece, in 1984–85, was a bronze relief mural, *Mythic Messengers,* for Teleglobe Canada's head-quarters in Burnaby, near Vancouver (PLATE 162).

Expo 86 in Vancouver coincided with an obsession Bill Reid had developed for under-standing the Haida canoe as a paradigm of Haida culture. Its pivotal role was recognized by the Reverend William Collison, who titled his reminiscences of the first mission to the Haida *In the Wake of the War Canoe* (see Lillard 1981). Reid was commissioned to carve and paint a 15-m (50-foot) war canoe from a red cedar log for the world's fair. He agreed to recreate this

PLATE 161
A portion of the Haida village reconstruction created by Bill Reid for the University of British Columbia Museum of Anthropology in Vancouver. *Photograph by George MacDonald, 1968. Author's collection*

PLATE 162

PLATE 162

Mythic Messengers is the title given by Bill Reid to his high relief bronze sculpture that combines figures from such classic Haida myths as the Bear Mother, the Dogfish Woman, the Eagle Prince and others. This version was donated to the Canadian Museum of Civilization by Teleglobe Canada. CMC (s89-4183)

PLATE 163 (facing page)

This gold saltbox portraying the Bear Mother myth was commissioned by the Canadian Museum of Civilization from Bill Reid in 1972. The Bear who abducted and married the woman is depicted on the box, while she suckles her two cubs on the lid. CMC IV-B-1574 (s83-368)

canoe, which he named *Lootas* (or *Wave Eater*), for the Canadian Museum of Civilization in fibreglass to permit its outdoor display. Each new canoe was to be the alter ego of the other: one was to have primary formlines in black, the other in red. Consequently, one canoe became known as *Black Eagle* while the other was known as *Red Raven*.

The pièce de résistance of Bill Reid's work is surely *The Spirit of Haida Gwaii*, commissioned by the firm of R. J. Reynolds for the new Canadian Embassy in Washington, D.C. This massive sculpture, which took more than three years to execute and resulted in a price tag of $1.8 million, was unveiled in 1992. The plaster pattern for the bronze cast was a perfect complement to the baroque plaster interiors that architect Douglas Cardinal had created for the new Canadian Museum of Civilization (PLATE 160). Long before the completion and opening of the museum in 1989, I had suggested to Maury and Mary Young of Vancouver, the eventual donors, that *The Spirit of Haida Gwaii* would be the crowning piece in the Grand Hall, signalling that Northwest Coast native culture was not extinct but was, shaman-like, rising from the ashes.

ROBERT DAVIDSON

The next generation of Haida artists is represented by Robert Davidson. In 1966, Bill Reid introduced himself to the young Robert Davidson, who was conducting a carving demonstration at a department store in Vancouver. At the age of twenty, Davidson began an eighteen-month apprenticeship with Reid, then continued his education at the Emily Carr College of Art and Design. A few years later, he was already distinguishing himself as a thoughtful and talented artist. Much has been written about his maturation as one of the new master artists of the Haida tradition (Halpin 1979, Stewart 1979, Thom 1993, Steltzer and Davidson 1994).

PLATE 164

The housefront carved and painted by Robert Davidson for the National Historic Sites and Monuments Board of Canada and the Old Masset Village Council in memory of the great artist Charles Edenshaw (Tahayren). The Frog design is based on a chief's seat carved by Charles Edenshaw. *Photograph by George MacDonald, 1978. Author's collection*

PLATE 165

Robert Davidson's gilded bronze sculpture representing Raven (in bas-relief on the rim) bringing light to humankind. The work was commissioned by Dr. Margaret Hess of Calgary for the Grand Hall of the Canadian Museum of Civilization. CMC VII-B-1822 (s89-1738)

One of the early features of Robert Davidson's work was the fact that he was rooted in the Haida community of Masset where he had spent his early years. Through his grandmother Florence Edenshaw Davidson, he was linked to artists Charles Edenshaw and Albert Edward Edenshaw. His grandfather Robert Davidson Sr. was a carver and a hereditary chief of the town of Kayung, and his father, Claude Davidson, was a carver who inspired his sons Robert and Reg (who is an artist in his own right) to express their heritage through art and other cultural activities, including dancing.

Robert Davidson's period of apprenticeship was brief, and he mastered much of the sophistication of Haida art in his twenties. He carved a totem pole for the village of Masset and, encouraged and aided by his family, raised it with appropriate ceremonies in 1969. A series of exquisite prints in the 1970s expanded his reputation, and in 1978 he completed a commission from the National Historic Sites and Monuments Board of Canada to create a distinctive memorial to Charles Edenshaw, who had been declared an artist of national significance (PLATE 164). Unfortunately, the traditional Haida house with its carved and painted memorial housefront burned to the ground a year later.

A commission in 1984 from the Maclean Hunter Company for its new headquarters in Toronto resulted in possibly the oddest pole raising on record. The triple *Three Watchmen* pole was lowered into place in an atrium by a 15-storey crane from the sky world (Steltzer and Davidson 1994:80). In 1986, the Pepsi-Cola company commissioned a set of three poles called *Three Variations on Killer Whale Myths* for its international sculpture park outside New York City (Steltzer and Davidson:83–84).

The apogee of Robert Davidson's art is possibly the large gilded bronze sculpture *Raven Bringing Light to the World*—over a metre (3 feet) in diameter—commissioned by Dr. Margaret Hess of Calgary in honour of the dedication of the Grand Hall at the Canadian Museum of Civilization in 1986. In this piece, the humanlike face that simultaneously represents the sun, the moon and the stars contrasts effectively with the encircling bas-relief design of the Raven with his all-devouring beak holding the combined celestial bodies (PLATE 165).

In 1994, the Canadian Museum of Civilization co-sponsored a retrospective exhibit, "Eagle of the Dawn," that brought together three decades of Robert Davidson's work and filled 930 m² (10,000 square feet) of exhibition space. He continues to work in gold and silver, as well as creating masks and prints and undertaking commissions for monumental sculptures. The fact that Robert Davidson is only slighter older now than Bill Reid was when he began to create art in the Haida style suggests that Davidson has many further contributions to make.

JIM HART

The youngest of the Haida carvers to show great promise is Jim Hart, who in 1988 supervised the construction of the Haida house in the Grand Hall of the Canadian Museum of Civilization (PLATE 86). He was born in Masset and is a descendant of the famous shaman Dr. Kudé. Jim Hart apprenticed with Bill Reid on the monumental sculpture *The Raven and the First Men.* Previously, he had worked with Robert Davidson on the Charles Edenshaw Memorial Longhouse.

During his early years as an artist, Jim Hart exercised his skills in many media, including silver and gold jewellery, and prints that explore the range of supernatural and human beings that are appropriate to his family. He also carved a replica of a pole that once stood at Masset in the last century and that now graces the outdoor Haida village at the Museum of Anthropology at the University of British Columbia. A bronze miniature of this pole stands as a tribute to the pioneer ethnologist Marius Barbeau in the salon named after him at the Canadian Museum of Civilization.

In 1993, the Canadian Museum of Civilization commissioned Jim Hart to create a *manda'a* figure, whose traditional purpose was to support the coffin of a Haida chief (PLATE 166). This sculpture takes its inspiration from a piece collected from Skedans by Charles F. Newcombe for the Field Museum, but Hart has embellished it with his own distinctive designs on the tail. The idea for this commission rose from the popularity of the *manda'a* figure of a Wasgo (or Sea Wolf) that Bill Reid carved for the Museum of Anthropology in 1964, based on a nineteenth-century one by Charles Edenshaw at the Royal British Columbia Museum.

Another challenge undertaken by Jim Hart was recreating on a monumental scale a small shamanic piece depicting a man and woman straddling a huge Frog carved by an unnamed master of Haida art, probably in the 1870s. This unknown artist is probably the author of a piece acquired by the Glenbow Museum from a New York collection in 1975, depicting a Chinese immigrant with a prominent queue and typical costume of the period, as well as a secret society headpiece (VII-B-110) in the collections of the Canadian Museum of Civilization. Jim Hart finished the tribute to the unknown artist early in 1995.

At an impressive potlatch held in Masset in 1995, the current Chief Edenshaw (Morris White) designated Jim Hart as his heir to his title.

THE NEXT GENERATION

The Haida now regard their future with hope, bolstered by recent developments that hold great potential for reinforcing their cultural revival. The first is the declaration of the islands of the South Moresby group of the Queen Charlotte Islands (Haida Gwaii) as a National Park focussed on the three ancient villages of Skedans, Tanu and Skungwai (Ninstints). Skungwai has in fact been recognized as a place of premier importance to the history of

humankind by the World Heritage Site Committee of UNESCO, although this declaration was never implemented because of its implications for Haida land claims. A group of young Haida who are concerned with their heritage as well as land claims began to control access to and protect the old village sites through an organization called Haida Gwaii Watchmen, whose headquarters are in Skidegate near the Queen Charlotte Islands Museum. Under the watchful eye of Gujao (Gary Edenshaw), this committee issues permits to people who wish to visit Skungwai (Ninstints) and other abandoned Haida village sites.

In 1991, the National Historic Sites and Monuments Board of Canada recognized the southern part of the Queen Charlotte Islands as Gwaii Hanas National Park. This zone includes the villages of Skedans, Tanu and Skungwai (Ninstints) as part of a Haida cultural landscape that should be protected from further clearcut logging activities. Parks Canada has worked out a joint agreement with the Haida Nation to protect the park's natural and cultural resources.

In the central area of Haida Gwaii, the village of Haina also has been declared a National Historic Site, and on the north coast, most of the villages including Kiusta, Yaku, Dadens and Yan are sites of National Historic Importance. Hectare for hectare, there are more aboriginal sites of National Historic Importance on Haida Gwaii than anywhere else in Canada. In Alaska, many of the Kaigani Haida village sites are protected within American national forest reserves.

The future of Haida art and culture appears to be in good hands with the current generation of talented artists, who are passing their skills on to yet another generation, contributing to the continuation of an art form that is as significant to the arts of humankind as those of ancient Egypt and China.

PLATE 166
This sculpture of a Beaver by Jim Hart is in the form of a traditional *manda'a*, or coffin support, used to display the burial chest of a high-ranking chief in his burial shed. Commissioned in 1993 by the Canadian Museum of Civilization for its Grand Hall and installed in 1995. CMC

BIBLIOGRAPHY

Barbeau, C. Marius. 1944. How the Raven Stole the Sun: Charles
   Edenshaw's Argillite Carvings. *Transactions of the Royal Society of
   Canada* 3rd series, vol. 38 (sect. 2): 59–69.

Barbeau, C. Marius. No date. Field notes, Queen Charlotte Islands.
   Barbeau Archive, Canadian Museum of Civilization, Hull, Quebec.

Barbeau, C. Marius. 1950. *Totem Poles* Vol. 1 and 2. National Museum
   of Canada Bulletin 119. Anthropological Series 30.

Barbeau, C. Marius. 1953. *Haida Myths Illustrated in Argillite Carvings.*
   National Museum of Canada Bulletin 127. Anthropological Series 32.

Barbeau, C. Marius. 1957. *Haida Carvers in Argillite.* Anthropological
   Series 38, National Museum of Canada Bulletin 139.

Beaglehole, John C., ed. 1955. *The Journals of Captain James Cook on His
   Voyages of Discovery.* 5 Vols. Vol.3: *Voyage of the Resolution and
   Discovery, 1776–1780,* 2 Parts. Cambridge, England: Published for the
   Hakluyt Society at the University Press.

Blackman, Margaret B. 1982. *During My Time: Florence Edenshaw
   Davidson, a Haida Woman.* Seattle: University of Washington Press;
   Vancouver: Douglas & McIntyre.

Blackman, Margaret B. 1990. Haida: Traditional Culture in *Handbook
   of North American Indians,* Vol. 7, *The Northwest Coast.* Washington:
   Smithsonian Institution. Pp. 240–60.

Boas, Franz. 1916. *Tsimshian Mythology* (based on texts recorded by
   Henry W. Tate). Bureau of American Ethnology Thirty-first Annual
   Report. Washington, D.C. (Reprinted New York: Johnson Reprint
   Corp., 1970.)

Boas, Franz. 1927. *Primitive Art.* Oslo: Instituttet for Sammenlignende
   Kulturforskning. (Reprinted: New York, Dover Publications, 1955.)

Boelscher, Marianne. 1988. *The Curtain Within: Haida Social and
   Mythical Discourse.* Vancouver: University of British Columbia Press.

Borden, Charles E. 1982. Prehistoric Art of the Lower Fraser Region in
   Indian Art Traditions of the Northwest Coast, ed. R. L. Carlson. Burnaby,
   B.C.: Archaeology Press, Simon Fraser University. Pp. 131–65.

Brink, Jacob H. van den. 1974. *The Haida Indians: Cultural Change
   Mainly Between 1876–1970.* Monographs and Theoretical Studies in
   Sociology and Anthropology in Honour of Nels Anderson,
   Publication 8. Leiden, The Netherlands: E. J. Brill.

Chittenden, Newton H. 1884. *Hyda Land and People: Official Report of
   the Exploration of the Queen Charlotte Islands for the Government of
   British Columbia.* Victoria.

Cole, Douglas, and Bradley Lockner. 1989. *The Journals of George M.
   Dawson: British Columbia, 1875–1878.* Vancouver: University of British
   Columbia Press.

Curtis, Edward. 1916. *The North American Indian,* Vol. 11, *The Nootka,
   The Haida.* Norwood, Mass.: Plimpton Press. (Reprinted New York:
   Johnson Reprint Corp, 1970.)

Dalzell, Kathleen E. 1968. *The Queen Charlotte Islands, 1744–1966.*
   Terrace, B.C.: C. M. Adam.

Dalzell, Kathleen E. 1973. *The Queen Charlotte Islands,* Book 2, *Places
   and Names.* Prince Rupert: Cove Press.

Davidson, Susan J. T. 1967. The Life and Work of Charles Edenshaw: A
   Study of Innovation. M.A. thesis, Department of Anthropology and
   Sociology, University of British Columbia. Pp. 1–71.

Dawson, George M. 1880. On the Haida Indians of the Queen
   Charlotte Islands. Appendix A in Reports of Explorations and
   Surveys, Report of Progress for 1878–79. Geological Survey of Canada.
   Montreal. Dawson Brothers. Pp. 103-175.

Deans, James. 1899. *Tales from the Totems of the Hidery,* ed. Oscar L.
   Triggs. Vol. 2. Chicago: Archives of the International Folk-Lore
   Association.

Dixon, George. 1789. *A Voyage Round the World: But More Particularly
   to the North-west Coast of America Performed in 1785, 1786, 1787, and
   1788, in the King George and Queen Charlotte . . .* London: George
   Goulding. (Reprinted New York: Bibliotheca Australiana No. 37, Da
   Capo Press, 1968.)

Dorsey, George A. 1897. A Cruise Among Haida and Tlingit Villages About Dixon Entrance. *Appleton's Popular Science Monthly* LIII(13):160–74.

Drew, Leslie, and Douglas Wilson. 1980. *Argillite Art of the Haida*. North Vancouver: Hancock House.

Duff, Wilson, and Michael Kew. 1958. Anthony Island: A Home of the Haidas in *British Columbia Provincial Museum of Natural History and Anthropology, Report for the Year 1957*. Pp. 37–64.

Dunn, John. 1844. *History of the Oregon Territory and the British North America Furtrade*. London.

Emmons, George T. No date. Catalogue records, National Museum of the American Indian (Heye Foundation), Bronx, New York.

Emmons, George T. 1907. *The Chilkat Blanket, with Notes on the Blanket by Franz Boas*. American Museum of Natural History Memoirs 3(4):329–401.

Emmons, George T. 1916. The Whale House of the Chilkat in *Anthropological Papers of the American Museum of Natural History* 19(1):1–33.

Fladmark, Knut R. 1973. The Richardson Ranch Site, A 19th-Century Haida House in *Historical Archaeology in Northwestern North America*. R. M. Getty and K. R. Fladmark eds. Calgary, Alta.: University of Calgary Archaeological Association. Pp. 53–96.

Fladmark, Knut R. 1978. The Feasibility of the Northwest Coast as a Migration Route for Early Man in *Early Man in America from a Circum-Polar Perspective*, ed. A. L. Bryan. Edmonton: Department of Anthropology, University of Alberta.

Fladmark, Knut R. 1989. The Native Culture History of the Queen Charlotte Islands in *The Outer Shore*, ed. Geoffrey Scudder and Nicholas Gessler. Queen Charlotte City, B.C.: Queen Charlotte Islands Museum.

Gessler, Trisha. 1971. A Stylistic Analysis of Twelve Haida Drawings in *Syesis* 4(1–2):245–252.

Green, Jonathan S. 1915. *Journal of a Tour on the North West Coast of America in the Year 1829; Containing a Description of a Part of Oregon, California and the North West Coast and the Numbers, Manners and Customs of the Native Tribes*. (Reprinted New York, Heartman's Historical Series, 1915.)

Halpin, Marjorie. 1979. Beyond Nostalgia: The Graphic Art of Robert Davidson in *Vanguard* 8:6.

Harrison, Charles. 1925. *Ancient Warriors of the North Pacific: The Haidas, Their Laws, Customs and Legends, with Some Historical Account of the Queen Charlotte Islands*. London: H. F. and G. Witherby.

Henderson, John R. 1974. Missionary Influences on the Haida Settlement and Subsistence Pattern, 1876–1920 in *Ethnohistory* 21(4):303–16.

Herem, Barry. 1990. A Historic Tlingit Artist: The Trail of His Work and Its Modern Re-Creation in *American Indian Art* (Summer): 48–55.

Hobler, Philip M. 1978. The Relationship of Archaeological Sites to Sea Levels on Moresby Island, Queen Charlotte Islands in *Canadian Journal of Archaeology* 2:1–13.

Holm, Bill. 1965. *Northwest Coast Indian Art: An Analysis of Form*. Thomas Burke Memorial Washington State Museum, Monograph 1. Seattle: University of Washington Press; Vancouver: Douglas & McIntyre. (Reprinted 1970.)

Holm, Bill. 1974. Structure and Design in *Boxes and Bowls: Decorated Containers by Nineteenth-century Haida, Tlingit, Bella Bella, and Tsimshian Indian Artists*. Washington: Smithsonian Institution Press. Pp. 20–32.

Holm, Bill. 1981. Will the Real Charles Edenshaw Please Stand Up? The Problem of Attribution in Northwest Coast Indian Art in *The World Is As Sharp As a Knife: An Anthology in Honour of Wilson Duff*, ed. David N. Abbott. Victoria: British Columbia Provincial Museum. Pp. 175–200.

Holm, Bill. 1982. *Soft Gold: The Fur Trade and Cultural Exchange on the Northwest Coast of America*. Portland: Oregon Historical Society.

Holm, Bill. 1990. Art in *Handbook of North American Indians*, Vol. 7, *The Northwest Coast*. Washington: Smithsonian Institution. Pp. 602–32.

Hoover, Alan L. 1983. Charles Edenshaw and the Creation of Human Beings in *American Indian Art Magazine* 8(3): 62–67, 80.

Hoover, Alan L. 1995. Charles Edenshaw: His Art and Audience. *American Indian Art Magazine* Summer 1995: 44–53.

Howay, F. W. 1929. The Ballad of the Bold Northwest Man: An Incident in the Life of Captain John Kendrick in *Washington Historical Quarterly* 20:114–23.

Inglis, Richard I. 1976. Wet site distribution—the northern case, Gbto33, The Lachane Site in *The Excavation of Water-saturated Archaeological Sites (Wet Sites) on the Northwest Coast of North America*, ed. Dale Croes. National Museums of Canada Mercury Series 50, Archaeological Survey of Canada Paper 50. Pp. 158–85.

Inverarity, Robert B. 1932. ms, Field Notes of a Cruise to the Queen Charlotte Islands in 1932. Personal archives.

Jackman, S. W. 1978. *The Journal of William Sturgis.* Victoria: Sono Nis Press.

Jenness, Diamond. 1934. Indian Vikings of the North West Coast in *Canadian Geographical Journal* VIII(5):225–46.

Jonaitis, Aldona. 1981. *Tlingit Halibut Hooks: An Analysis of the Visual Symbols of the Rite of Passage.* New York: American Museum of Natural History.

Jonaitis, Aldona. 1993. The History of Haida Art in *Robert Davidson: Eagle of the Dawn,* ed. Ian M. Thom. Vancouver: Douglas & McIntyre; Seattle: University of Washington Press.

Kaplanoff, Mark D., ed. 1971. *Journal of the Brigantine Hope on a Voyage to the Northwest Coast of North America, 1790–1792,* Joseph Ingraham. Barre, Mass.: Imprint Society.

Lillard, Charles. 1981. Edited and annotation edition of *In the Wake of the War Canoe* by William Henry Collison. Victoria: Sono Nis Press.

MacDonald, George F. No date. Field notes 1978, Kitsilas Canyon Project. Archaeological Survey of Canada, Canadian Museum of Civilization, Hull, Quebec.

MacDonald, George F. 1981. Cosmic Equations in Northwest Coast Indian Art in *The World Is As Sharp As a Knife: An Anthology in Honour of Wilson Duff,* ed. Donald N. Abbott. Victoria: British Columbia Provincial Museum.

MacDonald, George F. 1983. *Haida Monumental Art: Villages of the Queen Charlotte Islands.* Vancouver: University of British Columbia Press.

MacDonald, George F., and Jerome Cybulski. 1973. *Haida Burial Practices: Three Archaeological Examples,* Archaeological Survey of Canada Paper, Mercury Series 9. Ottawa: National Museum of Man.

MacDonald, George F., and Richard Inglis. 1981. An Overview of the North Coast Prehistory Project in *BC Studies* Special Issue 48:37–63.

McDonald, Lucile. 1972. *Swan Among the Indians: Life of James G. Swan 1818–1900; Based Upon Swan's Hitherto Unpublished Diaries and Journals.* Portland, Oregon: Binfords and Mort.

McKenzie, Alexander. 1891. Descriptive Notes on Certain Implements, Weapons, Etc. from Graham Island, *Royal Society of Canada, Proceedings and Transactions* 9, part 2:45–59.

Macnair, Peter L., and Alan L. Hoover. 1984. *The Magic Leaves: A History of Haida Argillite Carving.* Special Publication 7. Victoria: British Columbia Provincial Museum.

Newcombe, Charles F. mss by year and notes. Royal British Columbia Museum, Victoria, B.C.

Niblack, Albert P. 1890. *The Coast Indians of Southern Alaska and Northern British Columbia.* Annual Report of the U.S. National Museum for 1888. (Reprinted New York: Johnson Reprint Corp., 1970.)

Poole, Francis. 1872. *Queen Charlotte Islands: A Narrative of Discovery and Adventure in the North Pacific,* ed. John W. London. London: Hurst and Blackett. (Reprinted Vancouver: J. J. Douglas, 1972.)

Roquefeuil, M. Camille de. 1823. *A Voyage Round the World Between the Years 1816–1819 in the ship Le Bordelais.* London: Sir R. Phillips and Co.

Royal Anthropological Institute News April 1980 (37)1.

Severs, Patricia. 1974. Archaeological Investigations at Blue Jackets Creek, FlUa-4, Queen Charlotte Islands, British Columbia, 1973 in *Canadian Archaeological Association Bulletin* 6:163–205.

Shadbolt, Doris. 1986. *Bill Reid.* Vancouver: Douglas & McIntyre; Seattle: University of Washington Press.

Sheehan, Carol. 1981. *Pipes That Won't Smoke; Coal That Won't Burn: Haida Sculpture in Argillite.* Calgary, Alta.: Glenbow Museum.

Smith, Harlan I. 1919. ms, Archaeological Expedition to the Queen Charlotte Islands. Canadian Museum of Civilization, Hull, Quebec.

Stearns, Mary Lee. 1981. *Haida Culture in Custody, the Masset Band.* Seattle: University of Washington Press; Vancouver: Douglas & McIntyre.

Steltzer, Ulli, and Robert Davidson. 1994. *Eagle Transforming: The Art of Robert Davidson.* Vancouver: Douglas & McIntyre; Seattle: University of Washington Press.

Stewart, Hilary. 1979. *Robert Davidson: Haida Printmaker.* Vancouver: Douglas & McIntyre.

Sutherland, Patricia C. 1980. Understanding Cultural Relationships Across Hecate Strait, Northern British Columbia. Paper presented at the 13th Annual Meeting, Canadian Archaeological Association, Saskatoon, Saskatchewan.

Swan, James G. 1874. The Haidah Indians of Queen Charlotte's Island, British Columbia. With a Brief Description of Their Carvings, Tattoo Designs, etc. *Smithsonian Contributions to Knowledge* 21(4):1–15. (Reprinted Seattle: Shorey Book Store, 1964.)

Swan, James G. 1883. Journal of a Trip to Queen Charlotte Islands, B.C. Microfilm. Suzallo Library, University of Washington, Seattle.

Swan, James G. 1893. ms, Order of the houses as they used to stand at

Skidegate in 1893. Department of Anthropology, Field Museum, Chicago.

Swanton, John R. 1905. *Contributions to the Ethnology of the Haida.* Publications of the Jesup North Pacific Expedition 5(1); American Museum of Natural History Memoirs 8(1). Leiden: E. J. Brill; New York: G. E. Stechert.

Swanton, John R. 1905A. *Haida Texts and Myths: Skidegate Dialect.* Bureau of American Ethnology Bulletin 29. Washington, D.C.: Government Printing Office.

Thom, Ian M., ed. 1993. The Evolution of an Artist in *Robert Davidson: Eagle of the Dawn.* Vancouver: Douglas & McIntyre; Seattle: University of Washington Press.

Weber, Ronald. 1985. Photographs as Ethnographic Documents. *Arctic Anthropology* 22(1):67–78.

Wright, Robin K. 1985. Nineteenth-Century Haida Argillite Pipe Carvers: Stylistic Attribution. Ph.D. dissertation in Fine Arts, University of Washington, Seattle.

INDEX

Page references to captions are in *italic type*.

A

Adams, Chief Alfred, 214, 219
Angels, 205, *206*
Antkleg (Mike George), *195*
Archaeological sites, 4–6, *5*, 31, 37
Argillite carving, 9, 73, 94–97, *98, 115*, 159, *211, 213, 216, 219, 221, 221*
Armour, *136*, 137, *137*
Art
    flat design, 9–10, 12–13
    ledger drawings, 12
    North Coast art style, 9–12
    sale of, 9, 13, 27, 73, 94, 97, 98, 211
    sculpture, 13. *See also* Argillite carving;
        Poles, carved
Artists, 27, 97–98, *139*, 211–31. *See also* under
    individual names

B

Barbeau, Marius, 4, 172, 211, 225, 231
Basketry, 27–29, *27*, 127
Bear, *31, 39, 41, 63, 101, 133, 143*, 148, 172, 176, *184*, 188
Bear Mother saltbox, *226*
Beaver, 8, *28, 51, 80, 97*, 113, *115, 129, 143*, 172, *175, 233*
Beaver forehead mask, *80*
Beaver *manda'a, 233*
Birth charm, *53*
Black Canoe, The, 223
Black Eagle, 228
Blue Jackets Creek, 5–6
Boas, Franz, 67, 110–13, 118, 219
Bowls, 37, 43–44, *43, 44. See also* Dishes
Boxes, bentwood, 9, 12. *See also* Chests,
    bentwood
    food storage, 118, *118*
    making, 37, 44
    shaman's *55, 65*
    storage, 118, *120, 123, 206*
Breastplates, 137, *137*

Brink, Jacob H. van den, 136
Burial chests. *See* Chests, bentwood
Button blankets, 19–23, *21, 23, 206*

C

Canoes, 4, 5, 131–33, *131, 133, 134, 135, 225–28*
Canoes, models of, 131, *131*
Capes, painted leather, 16–19, *19*
Carr, Emily, 160
Cedar bark, 16, 118. *See also* Basketry
Cha'atl, 155, 157, 159–160, *160*
Chapman, Isaac (Ben), 219
Charles Edenshaw Memorial, *228*, 230, 231
Charms, *53, 55*, 57, *60, 65*
Chests, bentwood. *See also* Boxes, bentwood
    burial, 13, 103, *103, 125*, 127, *128, 129, 143, 150, 206*
    storage, *11*, 118–27, *123, 127*
Chief
    rank of, 7, 67, 101, 102
    regalia of, *15*, 15–35, 118
Chief's House, *167*
Chief's seat, 117, *155*
Chilkat blankets, *vi*, 15, 16, *16*, 31, 150, *188, 195*
Chittenden, Newton H., 7, 139, 166, 174
Cloak Bay, 139
Clothing, 16. *See also* Regalia
Coffin support. *See Manda'a*
Cojo, Eddie, *195*
Collison, Matthew, *195*
Collison, Rev. William H., 97, *103*, 164–65, 183–89, *195*, 225
Cook, Captain James, 16
Copper shields, 9, 15, *15*, 31–33, *34, 35, 143*, 148, 187, *206, 214*
Cosmology, 23–27, 33, 94, 102–3
Cowhoe, 164
Crest helmets, 197
Crests, 7–8, 16, 19, 110
Cross, John, 8, 12, 98, 221
Cumshewa, 154, *154*
Cumshewa, Chief, 154
Cunnyha, Chief (Gunia), 171, 209

Curtis, Edward, 67, 69, 71
Czar of Russia, 199

D

Dadens, 192, 214, 233
Dance aprons, 19
Dance ornaments, *68*
Dance wands, 57, *65*
Dancing spears, *68*
Davidson, Alfred, 131–33, *134, 135*
Davidson, Claude, 230
Davidson, Florence Edenshaw, 27, 219, 231
Davidson, Reg, 12–13, 230
Davidson, Robert, 13, 101, 127, 228–30, *228*, 231
Davidson, Robert, Sr., 131–33, *134*, 230
Dawson, George M., 110, 118, 145, *145*, 148, 150, 154, 157, 165–66, 174, 183
Deans, James, 3–4, *60, 101*, 105, 162–63, *164*
Deasey, Thomas, 98, *211*, 219
de Roquefeuil, Lieutenant Camille, 180–83
Dishes, *31*, 43–44, *43, 44. See also* Bowls
    bentwood, 37, 44, *46, 47, 48, 50, 51*
Dixon, Captain George, 162, 137, 171
Dogfish Woman frontlet, 27
Dolls, secret society, 77
Dorsey, George A., 174–77
Dossetter, Edward, 166, 178
Douglas, Governor James, 164, 174
Dragonfly, 94, 113, 192
Duff, Wilson, 5, *129*
Duncan, Ben, *195*
Duncan, Rev. William, 166, 184
Dunn, John, 183

E

Eagle, 8, *16, 21, 34, 86, 203, 206*
Eagle House, 208
Eagle House (later), 208
Eagle moiety, 6, 8
Easy to Enter House, 146, *146, 147*
Edenshaw, Amy, 214, 219
Edenshaw, Chief (first), 171, *172*, 190, 214

Edenshaw, Chief (Morris White), 231
Edenshaw, Chief Albert Edward, 33, 117, 136, 164, 171, 174, *175*, *176*, *177*, 183, 187–90, *190*, *195*, *200*, 211–16, *213*, *214*, 219, 230
Edenshaw, Charles (Tahayren), 7, 8, 12, 27, *28*, 54, 73, 98, *103*, 110, 113, 117, 118, *129*, 133, *134*, *135*, 171, *184*, 190, *190*, 211, *213*, 216, 219–21, *219*, *221*, 225, 230
Edenshaw, Gary (Gujao), 233
Edenshaw, George (Cowhoe), 164
Edenshaw, Henry, 117, 190, 192, *195*, 197, 214
Edenshaw, Isabella (née K'woiyang), 27, *28*, 219, 221
Edenshaw, Robert, *195*
Eleanora, 136
Emmons, George T., 11, 205
Epidemics, 13, 164, *172*

F
Feasts, 37, 43, 44, 164–65
Fishing, 4, 57, 139
Fladmark, Knut, 94
Flat design, 9–10, 12–13
Flicker House, *178*
Forehead masks, *80*
Fort Simpson, 94, 118, 160, 164, 183
Frontlets, 23–27, *23*, *27*
Furnishings, 117–27
Fur trade, 9, 19, 23, 94, 162–63, 164, 183

G
Gagiid, 71, *77*
Gambling, 93, *145*
Gambling sticks, set of, 93, *93*
Ganai, Chief, 157
George, Mike (Antkleg), *195*
Giatlins, Chief, *109*, 110, *169*, 216. *See also* Robson, John
Gida'nsta, Chief, 184. *See also* Skedans, Chief of
Gitkun, Chief, 140, 145, 146
Gladstone, Charles, 221
Gold, Chief, 107, *108*, 155, 157. *See also* Skotsgai, Chief
Gold, discovery of, 107, 155, *156*, 157, 164
Gold Harbour (Kaisun), 155. *See also* Kaisun
Gonankadet. *See* Konankada
Goose House, *180*
Graham Island, 3, *3*, 5–6, 139
Grant, Dorothy, 23, *23*, 127
Green, Rev. Jonathan, 97, 154, 163, 183, 209
Grizzly Bear, 8, *105*, *109*, *115*, 214
Grizzly Bear House, *vi*, *169*
Grizzly Bear-of-the-Sea, *195*

Grizzly Bear's Mouth House, *109*, 110, *129*, *169*, 216
Gujao (Gary Edenshaw), 233
Gulas, Chief, 174
Gunia, Chief, 171, 209
Gwaii Hanas National Park, 233
Gwaitilth, 54, 211

H
Haida Gwaii (Queen Charlotte Islands), 3, *3*, 139, 231–33
Haina (New Gold Harbour), *15*, 155, 157–59, *157*, *158*, 233
Hand maul, 101, *101*
Harrison, Rev. Charles, 57, *171*, 188
Hart, Jim, 190, 231, *233*
Hats, painted woven, 23, 27, *28*
Hawk, *46*, *148*
Head canoes, 131, *131*
Headdresses, 23–29. *See also* Helmets
Heiltsuk, *85*, 140
Helmets, *136*, 137, *137*
Hiellan, *190*, 191
Highest Peak in a Mountain Range, *15*
Holm, Bill, 12, 37, 108, *155*, 211, 223
House Always Looking for Visitors, 157–59
House for a Large Crowd of People, *190*
Housefront paintings, 105–10, *108*, *109*, *110*, *203*, *228*
Households, 6–7
Housepits, 101, 102, 117, *187*, *195*, 197
Houses, 6, 101–17, 145, 183–34. *See also* under individual names
Houses, models of, 13, 105, *107*, *109*, 110, *110*, 113–17, *115*, 171, *184*, 216
House Standing Up, 197
House That Can Hold a Great Crowd of People, 174, *175*, *176*, 214
House That Wears a Tall Dance Hat, 180
House Upon Which Are Clouds, 155
House Upon Which Storm Clouds Make a Noise, 216
House Waiting for Property, *157*, 159
House Where People Always Want to Go, *15*
Howkan, 107, 199–205, *203*
Hudson's Bay Company, 19, 94, 160, 183, 190

I
Ice age, 3–4
Ildjiwas, Chief, *178*
Ingraham, Joseph, 154, 162, 163, 180
Inverarity, Robert Bruce, 150, 171–72
Itltini, Chief, 171

J
Jade Canoe, The, 223
Jefferson, C., 164
Jenness, Diamond, 133
Jonaitis, Aldona, 57

K
Kadjis-du-axtc, 208
Kaga, *175*
Kaigani Haida, 3, *3*, 19, *19*, 102, 110, *110*, 171, 174, 192–209, 233
Kaisun (Gold Harbour), 155, *156*, 157
Kasaan, 205–9, *205*
Kayung, 180, *180*
Killer Whale, 8, 16, *19*, 57, *58*, *68*, 71, 117, *117*. *See also* Whale
Killer Whale, 225
Killer Whale dorsal fin ornaments, *58*, *68*, *84*
Killer Whale mask, supernatural, *84*
Kitkatla, 148–50, *150*, 154
Kitkune, 146
Kiusta, 171–72, *172*, 174, 199, 233
Klinkwan, 190, 192–97, *192*, *195*
Klue, Chief, *46*, 140, 145, 150
Konankada, 11, *11*, 16, 19, 31, 67, 107, 113, 117, 118, *118*, 123
Koyah, Chief, 136, 140
Kudé, Dr., 54, 188, *188*, 231
Kung, 174–77, *175*, *176*
Kwakwaka'wakw, 9, 31, 67, 71, 162

L
Labrets, *73*, *75*
Ladles, 37
Lady Washington, 140
Leather capes, painted, 16–19, *19*
Ledger drawings, 12
Legaic, Chief, 113, 137, 214
Leggings, 19
Lightning House, 157, 159
Lineages, 6–7, 8
Lootas (Wave-Eater), 133, 228

M
McKenzie, Alexander, 33, 53–54, 57, 180
Manda'a, 105, 231, *233*
Marks, Gerry, 12
Marks, John, 219
Marmot mask, *79*
Masks, 33, *37*, 67, *67*, *73*, *75*, *77*, *79*, *80*, *83*, *84*, *85*, *86*, *88*, *90*, 171, 188
Master Gambler, 11
Master of Souls, 11

"Master of the Chicago Settee," 12, 107, *108, 146, 146, 155*
Masset, 178, 180–90, *183, 190*
Masset Inlet, 139
Mathers, Edward, 166
Mats, 127
Maul, hand, 101, *101*
Maynard, Richard, *vi,* 166, 180
Mikatla, Donald, *195*
Missionaries, 12, 13, 71, 154, 163, 166, *171,* 183, 188, *206*
Monster House (Na Yuans), 113, 183–84, *184, 187*
Moody, Rufus, 221
Moon, 23, *83, 85, 86*
Moon frontlet, 23
Moon-Hawk plaque, *108*
Moon House, 107, *108*
Moon masks, *83, 85, 86*
Moresby Island, 3, 231
Mortars, 94, *97, 98*
Mortuary box, *160,* 171
Mortuary houses, *103, 105*
Mosquito Hawk House, 164
Mosquito mask, *90*
Mountain Goat, 8, *19, 150, 175*
Mountain Hawk, *175*
Museum of Anthropology, 140, 225, *225,* 231
Mythic Messengers, 225, *226*
Myths
    Bear Mother, *39,* 192–97
    flood, 3–4, *199*
    lazy son-in-law, 180, *180, 200*
    Nansimget, *39, 41, 48*
    Qingi, 67–69, 113, *199*
    Raven, 7, 8, 101, 117

N
Names, 6, 23
Nanjingwas, Chief, 166, *167*
Nansimget. *See* Myths
Na'qadjut, Chief, 180
Nasank, *195*
Necklaces, charm, 57, *60*
Newcombe, Charles F., 43, 93, 113, 127, 155, 160, 180, 188, 219
New Gold Harbour. *See* Haina
Niblack, Ensign Albert, 101, 199, 205
Ninsingwas, Chief, 7
Ninstints. *See* Skungwai
Ninstints, Chief, 139, *139. See also* Price, Tom
Nisga'a, 15, 23, *27,* 57
North Coast art style, 9–12
Nuxalk, 148

P
Paint bags, *71*
Paintbrushes, *31*
Peace ceremony, 187–88
Pipes, 94–97, *94*
Poles, carved
    house frontal, 13, 37, *110,* 140, *157, 175, 176, 180, 190, 206*
    house posts, *vi,* 110, *112*
    interior central, 110, 113, *115,* 146, *146, 147, 172, 195*
    memorial, 15, 110, 166, *169,* 178, 190, *99, 200, 205, 214–16, 219*
    mortuary posts, *105,* 140, *154, 171–72, 172, 174–77*
Poles, model, *vi,* 13, 97, *98, 158,* 211, *211,* 221
Potlatch, 7, 23, 71, 137, 165–66, *195,* 197
Prehistory, 3–6
Price, Tom (Chief Ninstints), 8, 12, 27, *139, 171,* 211, *213*
Prince of Wales archipelago, 3, *3,* 192
Property House, 171, 190

Q
Qingi. *See* Myths
Queen Charlotte Islands (Haida Gwaii), 3, *3. See also* Haida Gwaii
Qwa'Kuna, 110, *169,* 216, 219

R
Rafters, *110, 115,* 117
Rattles
    Raven, 31, *33*
    shaman's, *55, 57, 60, 62, 63, 148*
Raven, 8, 16, *16, 23, 33, 39, 41, 58, 94, 98,* 110, *160, 167, 175, 203, 205, 225, 228*
Raven and the First Men, The, 225
Raven Bringing Light to the World, 228, 230
Raven moiety, 6, 8
Raven rattles, 31, *33*
Red Raven, 228
Regalia
    chief's, 15–27
    secret society, 68, *68,* 71, *171. See also* Masks
    shaman's, 54–67
Reid, Bill, 118, 133, 221, 223, 225–28, *226*
Robin, *60*
Robinson, George, 166
Robson, John (Chief Giatlins), 8, 12, *23,* 27, *109,* 110, *139, 169,* 216, *216,* 219
Russ, Amos, 110
Russian influence, *34,* 163, 192, 199–205, *206*

S
Saltbox, *226*
Scott, Eddie, *195*
Screens, interior, 113–17, *203*
Sculpin, 8, *34, 62, 63, 115, 197*
Sculpture, 13. *See also* Argillite carving; Poles, carved
Sea Grizzly Bear, *146, 203*
Seagull, *vi*
Seal, 43, *126*
Sea Lion, *43, 65, 112*
Seas, Chief of the, *71, 118*
Sea Wolf, *135, 175, 200. See also* Wasgo
Secret societies, 67–71, *171. See also* Masks
Shakes, Chief, 205, *206*
Shaman, 33, 53–67, 69–71, 133, 188, *188*
    carvings of, 54, *55, 57, 58, 158*
Shaman's
    box, *55, 58, 65*
    charms, *53, 55, 57, 60, 65*
    masks, 47, *47*
    mortuary, 13, 54, *58,* 177
    rattles, *55, 57, 60, 62, 63, 148*
    regalia, 54–67
Shell middens, 5–6, *5,* 31, 37
Skedans, 148–50, *150,* 231
Skedans, Chief of, *146,* 148, *150,* 231
Skidegate, 162–66, *169*
    model of, 105, *107*
Skidegate, Chief, 7, 105, *107,* 110, 162, 216, 219
Skidegate Inlet, 139
Skidegate the Great, 107, 162–63, 164, *167*
Skilgoldzo (Daniel Stanley), 219
Skotsgai, Chief, 155, *155,* 160. *See also* Gold, Chief
Skowl, Chief, 102, 110, 199, 205, *205, 206*
Skungo, *176*
Skungwai (Ninstints), 139–40, *139, 140,* 231–33
Slaves, 7, 33, *57,* 133, 183, *206*
Sledgehammer, 101, *102*
Smith, Harlan I., 5, *5,* 190
Smoke feasts, 94
Smokehole carvings, 117, *117*
Soapberry spoons, 37
Social organization, 6–7
Soni-hat, Chief, 208
Soul catchers, *55,* 57, *117*
Spirit of Haida Gwaii, The, 223, 228
Spoons, 37, *39, 41*
Sqilao, Chief, 190
Sqiltcange, *190, 191*
Stanley, Daniel (Skilgoldzo), 219
Steel House, *175*
Stevens, Tom, 110

Stiltla, Chief Simeon, 54, *58*, 73, *75*, 178, 184, 211, 219
Stone, 4, 94, *97*, *101*, *102*. *See also* Argillite carving
Story House, 171, 174, 214, 219
Sukkwan, 199, *200*
Susan Sturgis, 136, 178, *187*
Sutherland, Patricia (Severs), 6
Swan, James G., 107, 146
Swanton, John R., 5, 6, 8, 53, 54, *60*, 69–71, 110, 113, 137, 171, 199, 219, 225

T

Talking stick, 146, *147*
Tanu, 140–46, *145*, 231
Tattoos, 8, 12, *71*, *188*
Three Variations on Killer Whale Myths, 230
Three Watchmen, 230
Thunderbird, 31, *48, 71, 86, 102, 176, 195, 219*
Tlingit, 9, 11, 15, 16, 23, 67, 117, 137, 150, 192
Totem poles. *See* Poles, carved
Trade, 6, 9, 31, 118, 131, 139, 148–50, 154, 160, 162, 183

Transformation masks, *vi, 86*
Trays
  bentwood, 44
  woven, 27, *28*
Tsebassa, Chief, 148
Tsimshian, 9, 15, 16, 23, 31, 54, 57, 67, *67*, 71, *83*, 107, *117*, 133, *145*, 148–50, 162, 164, 184
Tunics, 19, *19*, 137, *137*

U

Ulala Society, 69–71
Undersea World, Chief of the. *See* Konankada

V

Vancouver, 171
Victoria, 164
Visors, 137, *137*

W

Wadatstaia, Chief, 160
War coat, 137, *137*
War daggers, *vi,* 137, 214
Warfare, 5, 31, 133–37

Wasgo, 105, 146, *200, 213, 216. See also* Sea Wolf
Wave-Eater (Lootas), 133, 228
Whale, *vi, 47, 48, 102, 188, 219. See also* Killer Whale
Whale House, 192, 208
Wiah, Chief, 107, 113, 136, *177*, 178, 180, 183–87, *187*, 188
Wiah, Chief Henry, 178, 188
Winter dances, 67, 69
Work, John, 154, 155, 159, 171, 177, 192, 199
Wright, Robin, 97

X

Xa'na, Chief, *vi*

Y

Yaku, *172*, 233
Yan, 178, *178*, 233
Yatze, 174, *175*, *177*
Yeoman, Don, 12
Young, Henry, 4